Contents

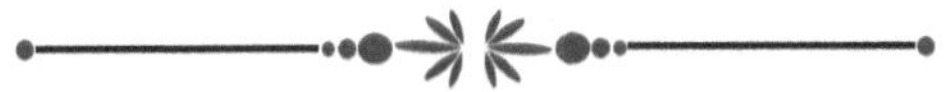

MANGO TO MAPLE

BEFORE YOU FLY FOR QUALITY OF LIFE

SHUCHITA SINGH

ISBN 979-8-89066-851-6

▪ CONTENTS ▪

Based on the author's experiences in Saskatoon.

Settling Abroad: The Dream of Every Indian

India is still called a 'developing nation'. This misleading notion is the reason millions of Indians dream of being in 'developed nations'. India was surely a developing nation 20 years ago, but the progress India has made in the last 20 years has allowed it to surpass well-established developed nations. And yet the perception still remains, the rumours still circulate—'the West is better'. The West does not want to accept that India has made progress, and India is living under the same delusion!

Every second home in India has family members who aspire to live a great life abroad. The specific country has to be decided but it must be one where life is valued and that has better facilities than those in India. A common notion is that humans are like insects in India. Their lives are not valued. If you value your life or want to be valued, move abroad.

It's impossible to go to a party that doesn't feature an uncle or aunty whose kid or whose uncle's uncle is living happily ever after abroad. Every office conversation must involve talk of a teammate moving abroad, to which you say, '*Mast ho gaya re iska!*[1] Lucky chap!' Every wedding is incomplete without the wait for the Canadian *bhai*[2] or Australian *buaji*.[3] It's completely normal to expect a grand gift from the NRI *mamu*[4] or *chachu*.[5] Nowadays, even your distant friend is likely to marry the person

---

1   'Good for them!'
2   Brother/cousin
3   Paternal aunt
4   Maternal uncle
5   Paternal uncle

they met while studying abroad. Every other kid is preparing for the IELTS and their parents are saving money in hopes of sending them abroad.

Because 'India is a developing nation'.

Favourite Destinations: US, UK, Canada, Australia

Usually, the destination is inspired by *maasi ki beti*[6] or Meerut *waali buaji*[7] or London *wale fufaji*.[8] The country in which your closest relatives reside is always the best one. As we only hear their stories, we assume that wherever they are is the best place to be—or else they wouldn't be there. The first impression of the country comes from *maasi ki beti* or London *wale fufaji ka* Facebook or Instagram account.

'What a view… What a trail… What a waterfall… What blue skies… What a shopping street… What a pizza… What a restroom…'

The never-ending list of 'What a…'

Then come their stories.

'There is a lot of pollution here… There in Canada, the air is sooo pure and fresh… Human life has no value in India, whereas Canada values human life… In Canada, everyone drives luxury cars…'

If we want to take a short cut, then we rely on the knowledge of our relatives. Otherwise, we start our own research.

Where should I go?

US → *Lots of money.*

UAE → *Lots of restrictions.*

---

6   Maternal aunt's daughter
7   Aunt from Meerut
8   Husband of paternal aunt from London

Australia → *Very good work-life balance.*

UK → *Not easy to get PR status.*

Canada → *Very easy to get PR status.*

People whose idea of life revolves around money run towards the United States, sometimes blackmailing their companies to secure a transfer. People who don't want to be too far from India go to the UAE. Australia is for people with a strong desire for 'work-life balance' and who are willing to put in a lot of effort towards securing their PR status. UK is usually the choice of people who get the chance to go there on a work visa.

Then, finally, comes Canada. '*Wahan to koi bhi ja saktha hai. Wo to sada Punjab hai ji.*'[9] People have this notion that moving to Canada is easy and anyone can do it.

---

9   'Anyone can go there, it's mini-Punjab.'

Canada: Land of Punjabis

As soon as we think of Canada, *dhol*[10] music starts playing in the background and we see a big sign that says:

Welcome to Canadda, *ji*!

Canada in two lines ® '*Bhaisaab* Canada *mein to Punjabi bhare pade hain! Wahan to* signboard *bhi Punjabi mai likhe hote hai!*'[11]

It was commonly believed that Punjab was a land of farmers, fields, festivities, rich food, and culture. But now it is seen as a land of 'immigrants'. The state has faced many hardships since its creation, from terrorism to drugs and now the brain drain. Every second house in Punjab has a few family members who live in Canada or plan to go to Canada. It's very common to sell one's fields and even one's house to collect money to leave for Canada. Everyone dreams of settling in Canada. So much so that it is now assumed that, for Punjabis, 'settling' means moving to Canada—they either become Canadians themselves or find a spouse who either is or plans to be settled in Canada. Let's not get into the number of scams that guarantee a sure-shot landing in Canada, covering everything from IELTS coaching to the issuance of study or work permits and even illegal border-crossings.

So the perception in India is that Canada is Punjab. But when you land in Canada, you realise that Gujaratis may be higher or equivalent in number there! Surprising? Well, perceptions can be misleading.

---

10 A large drum
11 Canada is full of Punjabi people. Even many of the signs in Canada are written in Punjabi.

Canada Through the Eyes of an Indian

For Indians who want to move abroad, Canada is the easiest destination. For some, it's a ladder to the US, but for most, it seems like a home away from home.

In India, Canada is seen as a country where no job is small or big. Everyone in Canada owns a luxury car, wears branded clothes and lives a luxury life.

Canada is a land of dreams that most people dream of. Here are some of the most common notions about Canada:

Household chores are a big problem in Canada—you have to do everything yourself. But, with time, you get used to of it and find your own ways of getting the work done. On the other hand, there are more advantages than disadvantages, like the pollution-free environment, crystal clear skies and beautiful greenery all over, all of which is a tonic for your health. The neighbourhoods are soooooo beautifully designed, it all looks all so dreamy... Also the education system in Canada is good and relaxed. Kids are not burdened with lots of homework or competition. In India, kids are stressed out, but in Canada they have the freedom to go beyond being a doctor or an engineer.

Apart from the problem of having to do household chores yourself, there is one more problem—finding a job in your stream. Initially, you have to struggle a lot to get a job, any job at all. You may need to do odd jobs, like delivery, being a cashier or being a salesperson or receptionist. You need to get certifications or licences in your stream to even become eligible to apply for jobs. But if you remain focused then you may be able to get a job that fits with your experience and past designation.

Canada maintains a very high quality when it comes to food. The fruits and vegetables there seem unreal in comparison to what we have in India.

Taxis are very expensive, so people prefer to use public transport.

Now, coming to the main thing for which Canada is famous—snow! Yes, snow is the game changer for people who consider or reject the idea of migrating to Canada. It's tooooo cold in Canada. But if you have the right gear and clothing, then you can go out even in -40 degrees. It's all about getting used to it. Wherever you live, you get used to the environment.

People chill during the summers and mostly remain outdoors, hitting trails, going hiking, visiting parks, lakes, and rivers and admiring and enjoying the natural beauty all over. Even during the winters, people are outside, playing winter sports. Winters do keep people indoors during spells of extreme temperature, but nothing stops. Canada remains functional as usual.

Canada is a multicultural land. There are people here from all parts of the world. There is cultural freedom and everyone lives happily without interfering in each other's lives. Rather, it's considered good to know people from every corner of world here. As a result, there is less racism in Canada than in other countries. People are very friendly and socially very outgoing, so you can mingle easily.

There is great scope for the enjoyment of your personal life here. Nobody at your office forces you to work overtime. Rather, professional life is quite chill. Nobody shares their personal number in the professional world, so it almost becomes impossible to reach you after office hours.

Even in your professional life, there is no stress. There are no hard deadlines. Everything is super cool and, once you have experienced working in Canada, you will make better progress in your career, as Canadian experience is preferred by companies. Of course, there will always be exceptions. Everything depends on the company, team or stream you work for or in, but, generally, things are chill here.

There are expenses, but, being Indian, we are able to handle them well.

In India, there is a huge difference between rent rates and EMIs or mortgage rates, but in Canada, they are both almost the same, so you can easily buy a home, although the scenario is changing slowly and the difference is increasing.

The medical system in Canada is quite a disappointment. It's very slow and time-consuming, but in case of an emergency, if you dial 911, the ambulance will be at your place in no time. You will even be airlifted if required. On the other hand, you will have to deal with long waiting periods if you need to see a specialist, like a gynaecologist or an orthopaedist.

The Day an Indian Decides to Emigrate

Watching your colleagues leaving the country one by one, tired of hearing elaborate stories from your London *wali bua* or Australia *wali chachi*,[12] frustrated by Instagram and Facebook statuses that say 'moving to…' and photos of hikes, bikes and lights posted by those who have already moved, finally you get fed up and start asking yourself, 'Am I the only one not worthy of being abroad? Why have I not moved?'

You try to convince your office first. You say to your manager, 'I will resign if you don't move me to the Mountain View office/the United Kingdom/our site in Australia.'

Your manager assures you that he or she will find you something.

You wait for one year… two years… and then finally decide that you must get a job that will send you abroad. You keep sending applications to various companies but none click.

So finally, you must hire a consultant to secure PR status. That's your last hope…

---

12 Aunt from Australia

The Endless Wait

You conduct an analysis to find a consultant with a 100% success rate and finally hire them. From that day begins your endless wait.

You keep gathering documents that you never valued, like your birth certificate. Apart from parents seeking to admit their children to nursery schools, does anyone know where anyone's birth certificate is? And if you are from an era in which no one had any birth certificates... welcome to the road of potholes. Now you have to seek out contacts in your birth city, which you have not visited in ages, to find someone to go to the municipality office and handle the formalities associated with 'non-availability of birth certificate'. You have to search for an acquaintance or relative who can help you.

You always had marksheets but never valued them. When you apply for a WES[13] (World Education Services) evaluation, you realise the value of your marksheets. If you have misplaced even a single marksheet, be prepared to reconnect with your college circle and go back to your college to fetch it. It doesn't matter if you live in Delhi and your college is in Chennai—you have to fetch it at any cost.

Then comes the next milestone: IELTS. Even if you are good at English, you will struggle to get a good score, and if you find English a bit difficult, then be prepared to climb Mount Everest. Let me give you

---

13 A nonprofit organization that provides credential evaluations for international students and immigrants planning to study or work in the US or Canada.

a piece of advice here: you can get a good IELTS score even if you don't know English. It's all about tips and tricks.

Finally, the day arrives. After putting in Herculean efforts, you have managed to collect all the required documents and secure a favourable WES evaluation and IELTS score, a process that may have taken as long as one or two years, depending on various circumstances, and you finally submit your application.

Oh, sorry, I forgot to mention an important thing: the PR application is a game of points. You have to score as many points as possible. If your points are sufficient, great, but if not, you have to repeat the process for your spouse as well to get enough points.

Once the application is filed, you are at the mercy of the Canadian application process. A series of twists and turns will follow, as you wait endlessly either to get an express entry invite or a provincial invite (which itself can take ages).

Once invited, you will be required to perform a series of tasks, including accepting the invite, getting a medical evaluation, and having your passport stamped. This seemingly short series may take anywhere between one and two years, with no way of tracking your progress apart from waiting and checking your email every day.

And don't forget, you will spend a lot of money at each stage of the process, roughly Rs 7–10 lakh in total for a family of four (two adults, two kids).

Before actually getting involved in the PR process, you might have known anxiety as the state that one experiences while waiting for Board results or watching their favourite football or cricket team play live. But as soon as you dive into the PR application process, anxiety becomes your permanent companion. A companion who never leaves your side… a companion in your sleep… a companion in your dreams… a companion who is not so friendly but accompanies you every morning and night… Anxiety becomes a synonym of breathing, with a slight difference: normally, you breathe in and out, but with anxiety, you always breathe in…

The Big Day: PR Approved

You get up and, not even having opened your eyes properly, you grab your phone and check your email. Disappointed, you put your phone back. You have gotten used to checking your email as soon as you get up, as Canada works when India sleeps. Each email you have received from IRCC (Immigration, Refugees and Citizenship Canada) so far has been sent when it is night in India. You hope that one fine morning you will get *the* good news.

And one fine morning you do. You see the email that you have been waiting for. You cannot believe it. Are you seriously looking at this email? You read it twice, thrice, go over its contents again and again, and take screenshots just in case something happens to it. You forward it to your spouse and your consultant and then you finally come to your senses and break the good news to your spouse in person. Both of you start jumping for joy, finally hopeful that you are at the end of your endless wait.

A new beginning. The beginning of your dreams coming true. You make a checklist of items to be taken along, items to be sold, and items to be transferred. You have to rent or sell your house, if you own one. Er… wait… you cannot start making the list yet. Even after you receive the PR invitation, the follow-up steps like medical passport stamping can take a year or two.

Oh gosh! Seriously? There's more waiting?

Wait… wait… wait… medical evaluation… wait… wait… wait…

… wait…

… wait…

… wait…

… wait…

… passport stamped…

Yessssss.

Please return to your list now.

The List

1. Items to be taken along.
2. Items to be left behind.
3. Items to be sold.
4. Items to be given to *mami,*[14] *chachi,*[15] etc.
5. Items to be purchased in Canada.
6. Items to shop for:

   - Luggage
   - Clothes
   - Essentials
   - Utensils
   - Farewell gifts

7. List of people to meet before departure.
8. House—to be rented or sold? Painted? Notice period?
9. Kids' school TCs.
10. Kids' books.[16]

---

14 Maternal aunt

15 Paternal aunt

16 Indians often carry Indian school textbooks with them, especially math and science textbooks, as the Canadian education system is different from the Indian system.

11. Book tickets—Air Canada? Air India?
12. Hand in notice at work.
13. Bank formalities.
14. Canadian banking.

    • Open account.
    • Transfer money.

15. Search for a house to rent.
16. Which city is to be the port of entry?
17. Which items are you allowed to carry through security checks and immigration when you fly?
18. How to take jewellery?
19. How to pack?
20. How to take all *bhagwaan jis*[17] along?
21. What to eat before departure?

Choose Haldiram's/MTR's ready-to-eat items.

Earlier you had anxiety, but now you have lost sleep. Everything is endless and the available time seems to be unreasonably limited, leading to chaos, with many tasks to be completed every day.

Now we come to the role of YouTube. You start exploring YouTube for each list item... and end up making lists of lists. You learn about all the channels related to immigration. You watch videos in which residents of Canada discuss their annoying day-to-day household problems as well to gain relevant information. YouTube becomes your educational institution, helping you make decisions about each item on the list. The list keeps growing and you keep trying to tick off all the items. You feel like you are running on a treadmill whose speed is increasing with every moment and like you may fall off at any moment.

---

17 Gods (idols)

Finally, there comes a day when you are done with most of the items on your list and you decide to compromise on some of the to-dos and accept the fact that you cannot cover everything.

Flight of Dreams

You now need to book your flights. The most important question: 'Which flight allows the maximum luggage? We will go in that one.'[18] When you need to restrict yourself to two bags of 23 kg each, when you need to pack roughly 30–40 years of love, life, and emotions into 46 kg, it becomes difficult to decide what to choose or leave. Everything, every single emotion, every single moment, seems important, seems like it should be taken along.

The home into which you have poured your blood and sweat… the home that you built over years… the home that you have endless memories of… you couldn't have imagined life without it, but now it needs to be abandoned. You struggle with the idea of just leaving it. The thought shakes you up… you experience bouts of sudden anger that are hard to understand. Is it the pain of leaving the life that you have lived until this point or the pain of choosing one thing over another? Again, you start questioning yourself.

Have I made the right decision? Do I need to leave all this that I have worked hard for years to earn?

Anyway, you cannot step back now. You don't have any choice but to move forward. Again, YouTube comes to the rescue. You go through all the pros and cons of flying Air India and flying Air Canada. Finally, after watching countless videos and calling the airlines' customer care helplines, you conclude that both airlines have the same weight limit for luggage. The choice is yours.

18

You don't have much choice, as only Air Canada and Air India have direct flights, which offer the shortest travel times. Finally, after many discussions with acquaintances in Canada and hours of YouTube videos, you book the flights. As soon as the flights are booked, you start to think that you have already landed in Canada. But, excuse me, there is still a long way to go.

You juggle completing the to-do list, handling emotional trauma, and the anxiety surrounding an uncertain future… You never liked your relatives much but suddenly you start recalling sweet memories with them… You make plans to meet them at least once before actually leaving and, during the last catch-up, you realise why you never liked them… It is like a spinning wheel that always stops at the same number.

A family of four needs eight large suitcases, the kind you've either never purchased before or maybe had just one of. Suddenly, it seems like the whole house is full of only suitcases. Once purchased, they're all over your home, and your home turns into a motel until the day of your departure. These suitcases remind you at every moment that you are going to fly soon, that you are going to abandon your house soon, that you are going to abandon your country soon…

If you have been doing well in India, that is, if you earn a decent salary and have been living a good life, well, I have some bad news for you. The more settled your life in India, the more anxiety you are going to experience during the 'yet to fly' phase.

You reach the point of actually needing to leave for the airport. The day for which you have been preparing is finally here. Heart uncontrollably beating, mind full of uncertainties, you take one last look at your beautiful abode of many years. A day of last hugs… a day of tears… a day of standing on the threshold of a new world…

Your life is about to change forever. You move the suitcases around with a heavy heart. You have nothing to say.

A trip to the airport has never taken so long. The parents and the friends who come to see you off at the airport seem to be your last *kadi* with India, which you have no choice but to break.

The final byes, the final cries, feel like they are taking your breath away. For moments, you feel like you cannot breathe. After several minutes of turmoil, you finally collect yourself. You are still waving to the people outside the airport. Your parents/relatives are standing outside, maybe still hoping that you will change your mind.

You keep your eyes on them for as long as possible, realising that you may not be able to see them again for a long time. Yes, I agree that WhatsApp video calls have shortened the distance between loved ones, but the distance still does exist. No technology can be a replacement for physical presence.

Slowly, you move towards the airline check-in counters, losing sight of your loved ones. Finally, you accept it. It's gone forever. You accept your destiny and move forward.

Completing the check-in process and the security and customs checks is like being in one of Rana Sanga's battles. Finally, you emerge victorious, successfully completing all the steps with no hiccups. There comes a sigh of relief—you didn't make any mistakes while booking the tickets. No issues with your visa. All the paperwork you have been carrying and protecting with your life and all your worrying and prayers to God seem to be working.

Boarding begins and so does the conversion of your dream into reality. Amidst the anxiety of the unknown, in-flight breakfasts and dinners seem tasteless! Though you are already flying, your mind is still occupied with thoughts about the immigration process. Though you have seen many videos, you still fear something going wrong somehow.

Finally, the tiring 17-hour journey comes to an end.

Canada: The Land of the Snowy Sun

You arrive at long last in 'the land of the snowy sun', the land of immigrants, the land of Punjabis, the land of Ferraris and Porches. Yes! Now you are 'abroad'. Immigration formalities take their own time, and as soon as they are completed, the immigration officer says, **'Welcome to Canada.'**

At that moment, you realise for the first time, **'Oh, I am in Canada.'** You have fulfilled your dream. You have been so busy with the nitty-gritties that you almost forgot to enjoy the moment!

Thus starts a journey of change… change at every step… change in the way you deal with people… change in the way you order food at a restaurant… change in how you spend…

* * *

The sky was the first thing that caught our attention at the airport. It seemed so blue and clear, as we remembered it being in our childhood and had seen it depicted in Hollywood movies.

We were breathing 100% pure oxygen. The AQI was less than ten. Yes, our lungs felt blessed, as, for the first time in ages, we were feeding them clean air.

Our lifeline, the mobile phone, needed a SIM change. We decided to sit in a coffee shop, grab some snacks and bring our phones back to life. We had started reading ingredients before ordering anything, as non-vegetarian food is common in Canada and vegetarian dishes are rare. It's like being a Jain in India—they don't eat onion or garlic and almost all the dishes in India have both. If you know that pain, you will be able to relate to the pain of being a vegetarian in a land of non-vegetarians.

Our options were limited to pizzas, fries, salads, donuts and muffins. We needed to serve ourselves, which is exactly the opposite of what we were used to, although we had experienced self-service occasionally, at Haldiram's or Bikanervala. We started missing those eateries. We also began to doubt our own English, which seemed fluent in India but was incomprehensible to most people abroad, so we had to go slow and repeat almost everything. Then we realised that Indians know far better English than we thought, but the way we speak is different.

When we went to the washroom, we encountered the worst nightmare of our lives, which we had expected but found hard to accept: using the loo without access to a jet spray. Don't worry, you'll get used to it or find a workaround. I can't go into too much detail, for obvious reasons.

After this chain of around seven changes, we finally replaced our SIMs. From Airtel to Rogers, or Vodafone to Fido, or Reliance to SaskTel. Welcome to Canada!

We had never carried so much luggage in our lives, so we kept counting our bags just to make sure we hadn't misplaced any. We needed to hire two big SUVs for our family of four. Finally, after a great deal of struggle, our luggage got loaded and we headed to the hotel that we had booked for a week, as people had told us that we would be able to find a home on rent, or rental, easily in that much time. Though we had the option of booking an Airbnb or finding rentals online, we wanted to be in the comfort of a hotel after such a long journey, so we said to ourselves, 'What is the point of having worked so much if I can't even allow myself this convenience?'

We landed on May 29, which is supposedly summer in Canada, but for us it was the equivalent of India's winters. We were wearing the jackets we had carried in our cabin baggage, knowing how cold it was going to be.

The journey from the airport to the hotel was tiring but we were thrilled, finding everything on the way beautiful. Our tiredness reached its peak but the blue sky, fresh air and beautiful structures around us made our day. Finally, we reached the hotel. Nobody helped us with our luggage. We had to fetch a trolley and transport it ourselves.

We checked into the hotel and asked the receptionist whether there was some space for our luggage, as we wouldn't be able to fit it all in a single room. Thankfully, they helped us store our luggage. It was already evening. I don't remember if we had eaten anything. As we have kids, we thought of getting milk, water, bread and some snacks. So we googled the closest 7/11, found one that was within walking distance and headed straight to it. I suppose it was already seven or eight p.m. The city looked beautiful and calm, but there wasn't a single human out and about.

Everything at the 7/11 seemed so new. There were so many flavours of milk—chocolate, strawberry, all sorts of coloured bottles. We grabbed what we needed and went back to the hotel. It was almost nine p.m. and there was still so much sunlight! The sun only set around ten p.m.! The phenomenon called jet leg hit us, and we slept. All through the next day, we sleeeeeeeeeept.

* * *

List of changes:

1. Sky.
2. Air.
3. SIM.

4. Reading ingredients: no red or green labels.
5. Self-service: food and luggage at hotels.
6. Doubts about your English: different ways of saying the same thing.
7. Loos without jet sprays.
8. Longer days: the sun sets at ten p.m. and rises at four a.m.
9. Realtors and brokers don't share their cell phone numbers (although this varies from city to city).
10. Brokers are not in a hurry to rent out properties.
11. Kids' holidays shift from May–June to July–August.
12. Medicines are not readily available.
13. You come closer to nature and start enjoying the sky, the air, the trees and rivers.
14. Press up to switch things on, press down to switch them off.
15. No drying of clothes outside—use a dryer.
16. Drink water directly from taps, unfiltered.
17. Get used to cold beverages in the freezing winter.
18. Dehydration needs to be taken seriously.
19. Get used to Gatorade/Gzero.
20. Coffee is the new tea.
21. Croissant is the new *samosa*.
22. Frozen food is not that bad.
23. Humidifiers are needed.
24. Be a DIY person for everything.
25. Keep all kinds of tools.
26. Milk packaging.
27. Milk flavours.
28. Prescriptions are not handed over to patients; rather, they are directly sent to pharmacies. You cannot take more medicines than prescribed. Drug stores take time to hand over medicines as they label each medicine with patients' details, dosage and side effects.

List of things no one told me about (possibly Saskatoon-specific):

1. All rental applications are online.
2. We were able to reach out to the MLA about the delay in the delivery of our PR cards.
3. We had to show brokers our bank balance and proof of employment. It's hard to rent if you're jobless.
4. People who are homeless mostly roam around or lie on the pavements downtown.
5. YouTube is not the ultimate truth. Start talking to people who actually live in the city you plan to move to.
6. Canada is expensive. It used to be affordable, but now you cannot buy a house at an EMI equivalent to rental rates anymore.
7. Not everyone owns luxury cars.
8. The process of searching for a home to rent varies from one province to another, but it seems the rental crisis is universal. Finding a house was hard in Saskatoon. Toronto is similar.

Our search for a rental started. I called rental companies over the next several days and asked about the availability of houses to rent. We would be out first thing in the morning and would spend the whole day looking at houses. Fortunately, we took cabs to save time, but had to spend quite a lot on the fares. Even though Saskatoon, the city we landed in, was not very large, cab journeys cost around $40–50.

We kept on looking at houses, unaware that **the correct way was to apply online, then talk to the broker and visit the house.** As nobody told us this, we ended up spending more time looking for a rental. Our preference was for condos or flats over independent houses, as we would experience Canada's winter for the first time and didn't want to deal with shovelling snow, for the first year at least. All the high-rise condos were downtown and nothing seemed satisfactory. We made and broke many deals in a short span of time, and even increased our budget from

$1,300 to $2,500. It was all super expensive. As brokers or realtors don't share their cell numbers, it was very hard to get in touch with them. We had to wait for our landline call to be transferred or try later. Email was the only channel of communication. It was another change for us to get used to that brokers were in no hurry to rent out their properties.

We finally got a condo with a covered garage, a patio and a beautiful view of Saskatchewan River. The location was beautiful and there would be no need for us to shovel snow. We had already extended our hotel stay from five to ten days in the absence of a rental, so we were very eager to shift to our new abode.

Oh, sorry, I forgot to describe our experience at the hotel while we were in search of a rental. For those 10 days, each morning we had a breakfast of toast, muffins, eggs, hash browns, waffles, yoghurt and Kellogg's cereal. Yes, I am not kidding. The menu was the same every day. There were several other items that we didn't eat, like bacon and scrambled eggs. Even though we were staying at one of the best four-star hotels in the city, we found ourselves yearning for India's hospitality and buffets, which led us to order from Indian restaurants. There were multiple options to choose from, so we never ended up missing Indian food. From day one, we were eating *dal makhani* and butter *paneer* with *naan*.[19]

Almost all the cab drivers came to know us, as we were hiring taxis all the time. The one very memorable driver we met was Garland. He was as good as his name, a genuine person who gave us a free, guided city tour and honest advice about everything whenever we were out with him. He was the one who introduced us to Swan Pizza, which serves the most delicious pizza. It's so loaded and fresh that even people who don't eat pizza start doing so when they go there. I definitely haven't had such pizza in India.

---

19 *Dal makhani*, butter *paneer* and *naan* are all popular north Indian food items.

Garland was the one who told us that the home we had chosen was not in a very good location and advised us to think about it. We knew the western part of the city was not ideal and it was better to rent a place on the eastern side, but we were unaware that even downtown was not a good area. We had heard on YouTube that downtown was where one should look for places to rent. This was how we realised that **not everything you hear on YouTube is true or trustworthy.**

Downtown is usually where homeless people reside and roam, so it seems insecure. The homeless never harm anyone, but they usually do drugs and can be seen lying unconscious or gathered in groups, which creates an unsafe atmosphere. We lived in the condo for three months and I never felt unsafe, but whether it's good or bad to live downtown depends on what you are used to and what you are looking for.

The park was right in front of our condo, and the kids enjoyed it and the view of the river just across the street. We too enjoyed the view, the vibe, the pure oxygen and the delayed sunsets. We used to sit for hours under the filtered, ultra-clean blue sky. When airplanes flew by, they were clearly visible and it always seemed like a miracle. We had gotten so used to grey skies and hazy views that I had never imagined the famous Microsoft Windows background of a green landscape and blue sky was a picture of the real world until I reached Canada.

Although we enjoyed our days at the condo, we had to look for a new house, as school was due to start in September and the one close to the condo, which fell on the western side of the city, was not good.

An Emergency

It was ten-thirty a.m. on July 9. I was taking a shower, the kids were watching TV and my husband Ashish was offering prayers. As soon as he was done, he knocked on the bathroom door.

'How much more time are you going to take?'

Assuming he was hungry, I hurried up. I emerged from the bathroom to find him in a weak and disoriented state.

'I am blacking out, not able to see anything. I am feeling very dizzy. I can't stand.' He fell onto the bed saying, 'I am vomitish.'

Suddenly, my head too started spinning. *Could it be a heart attack?* We were just 11 days old in Canada! Based on his condition, I thought perhaps his BP was shooting up, so I gave him my BP medicine, immediately called a taxi and left for the hospital with him. The kids were at home.

As soon as we reached the ER, we were asked to show our health cards and passports. Fortunately, I had a soft copy of my passport, which I showed them. But they hadn't yet touched or looked at Ashish. He was unable to stand due to his dizziness. I requested a wheelchair, made him sit and fetched a vomit bag. He started filling vomit bags. The situation was getting completely out of control.

Tears streamed out of my eyes. I requested the nurses to at least check his BP, sugar, etc. After multiple requests, they checked both very indifferently and asked us to wait. His condition was degrading with every second. He was unable to even sit and his head was spinning uncontrollably. I called Neeraj, a friend of mine in Toronto. He too was unable to help. He was aware that Canada's healthcare was broken and that, even in emergencies, people had to wait for hours. He consoled me, saying, 'Don't worry, I will fly there if needed.'

I then called a friend of ours in India who was an ENT specialist and described everything to him between bouts of tears. After listening to me, he told me not to worry and assured me that it had nothing to do with the heart and was most probably BPPV, a condition related to the ear. He told me to ask for an MRI to be conducted.

Lastly, I called up a friend of a friend who lived in Saskatoon. He arrived at the hospital and his stories of waiting for treatment gave me consolation. He told me of the time when his hand was burnt and he had had to wait four hours to see a doctor.

After two hours, we finally got a bed in a very small, partitioned room. A nurse performed an ECG and asked us to wait for the doctor.

Ashish's condition was terrible. Not a single nurse was around to attend to him. This put me in a dilemma—*should I go back to the kids, who are alone, or stay with Ashish?* We hadn't eaten anything since the morning, so I asked a nurse if there was anything he could eat. She brought him toast and juice, but Ashish could hardly eat anything.

I went searching for a vending machine, but unfortunately the one I found did not accept my card. A gentleman, observing my efforts for some time, asked me to let him try and managed to extract a Coke. I offered him cash as repayment, but he refused it and left. I guess I met an angel.

The wait for the doctor was getting unbearable and the kids were hungry, so I decided to go back and give the kids something to eat and settle them, as we didn't know how long it was going to take. I spent around 30 minutes with the kids, making sure they were comfortable and fed, before going back to the hospital. Finally, the doctor arrived and said that Ashish's problem seemed to be related to the ear—maybe an infection. He told us to do a blood test and then leave. Ashish was still dizzy, still vomiting, but the doctor said it was going to be like that for two or three months, after which he would be okay. Shocked and unable to think of anything, we left. Ashish was still filling bags with his vomit.

I was feeling helpless and was eager to do anything to make Ashish better. Suddenly, I recalled that the doctor had said, 'You should have gone to a walk-in clinic instead of coming here. You have wasted so much money by coming here.' I am not sure why he said that, as healthcare is free in Canada, but I decided to take his advice. I called several walk-in clinics and one agreed to see us.

We had to wait at the clinic for two more hours to be told again that it was something to do with the ears, but nobody recommended an MRI or a scan or anything. They just prescribed Ashish some medicines to relieve his dizziness. It was already nine p.m. We had been out since ten-thirty a.m.

We went to a drug store to get the medicines. There, we were told it would take another hour to get the medicines ready. We were in no condition to wait, so we arranged for home delivery the next day and went back home empty-handed.

My tears didn't stop the whole night. We blamed ourselves for the blunder we had made by moving to Canada. Suddenly, all the happiness of moving abroad vanished. We started missing the privilege that we had taken for granted back in India, of being able to approach a doctor at any time. Suddenly, the Indian medical system seemed far better. Though we always knew the difference between the medical systems of the two countries, we never imagined that it was this extreme.

Days passed and we kept going from one walk-in clinic to another, one physiotherapist to another. We even booked an appointment with an ENT specialist. MRIs and CT scans are so common in India that we never thought they were rare in other parts of the world. But yes, in Canada, MRIs and CT scans are rare.

When we visited the ENT specialist, he said, 'Everyone gets dizzy, it's very common and nothing abnormal. Your brain and nerves are okay and you don't have a medical condition. This will go away with time.'

All our hopes were shattered after this meeting. We felt helpless, as if we were stranded on an island.

Three months passed. We met several people and made friends with them. We also moved, overcoming our fear of shovelling snow, to an independent house in a neighbourhood where schools were good.

Basics of Canada

Health Card

Sample Health Card

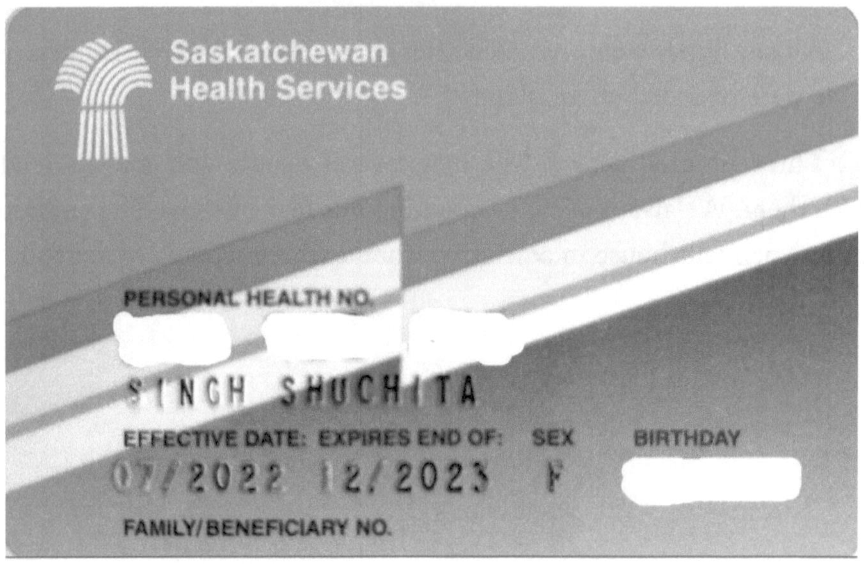

Your health card is your most important document in Canada. Each province (state) has its own health card, so if you move from one province to another, you need to re-apply for one.

The health card application process is entirely online. You simply need to go to the relevant website, create an account, upload your signed COPR (Confirmation of Permanent Residence) and then wait roughly three weeks. The waiting period depends on the province you are in.

If you are moving to Saskatchewan:

Apply for your health card @ https://skhealthcard.health.gov.sk.ca/

Access your health records @

https://www.ehealthask.ca/mysaskhealthRecord/MySask healthReacord/

One important point to note is that you cannot apply for a health card if you don't have an address, i.e. if you don't own a house or have a rental lease. So you must find yourself a home before applying for a health card.

Raise a query if the 'rough time' has passed. When we applied for our health cards, we waited for a long time without any updates. Only when we raised a query about not having received any health cards were we informed that our COPR documents had not been stamped by an immigration officer and therefore could not be processed. We then uploaded stamped copies and received our cards within the estimated time.

As discussed earlier, we had to deal with an emergency very early on, before we received our health cards. Let me explain how it works if you need to see a doctor without a health card.

If you go to an ER, you will be asked for your passport and it will then be noted that you are yet to receive your health card. The rest goes on as usual. The doctors and nurses attend to you as they would if you had a health card. You don't need to pay anything. But later, you receive a letter from the ER that specifies the bill amount and requests you to call the hospital and provide them with your health card number as soon as you receive it. You will keep receiving those until you provide the hospital with your health card details.

So we did update the hospital and then it was free. No extra amount had to be paid.

SASKATOON HEALTH REGION
Saskatoon City Hospital
701 Queen Street
Saskatoon, SK S7K 0M7
Tel. (306) 844-4252

INVOICE

Please detach this upper portion and return with your remittance.
Retain bottom portion for your records.
If you require a receipt, please check this box ☐

SHARMA, ASHISH

SASKATOON, SK S7M5M8

ID NO.	161912
INVOICE NUMBER	10879054
PATIENT NAME	SHARMA, ASHISH
TOTAL DUE	$1,011.00
AMOUNT PAID	$

SASKATOON HEALTH REGION
INVOICE

INVOICE #: 10879054
INVOICE DATE: 21 JUN 2022

START DATE	END DATE	ITEM DESCRIPTION	QTY	UNIT PRICE	EXTENDED AMOUNT
10 JUN 2022	10 JUN 2022	EMERGENCY	1	$1,011.00	$1,011.00

AMOUNT DUE UPON RECEIPT OF INVOICE: **$1,011.00**

Please let us know by calling (306) 844-4252 if you have a valid Health Coverage in another province. We will require your Health Card Number and the Expiry Date where applicable. Otherwise, your prompt payment is expected by return mail.

If you live in Saskatchewan and you want to renew your Health Card, please call the Ministry of Health at 1-306-787-3475.

Please quote your **Invoice Number** in your remittance

Your cheque should be made payable to: **SASKATOON HEALTH REGION**

Mail to: **Financial Services**
Saskatoon City Hospital
701 Queen Street
Saskatoon, SK S7K 0M7

To pay by credit card, call Cashiers at (306) 655-8783 between 7:30 am to 12:00 noon and 12:30 to 4:00 pm, Monday to Friday

NIC_INVOICE_NCAC

Page 1 of 1

Walk-in clinics are a bit different when it comes to payment. You need to pay their fees if you avail their services without a health card, but you are refunded as soon as you get a health card. What you need to do is go to the clinic you paid and tell them that you now have a health card.

Keep your payment receipt safe so that you can show it to them. The amount will be credited back to your card with a tap. So you actually lose nothing and pay no extra amount even when you are waiting for your health cards.

Now, after you get your health card, the next step is to assign yourself a 'family doctor'. A family doctor is a doctor who gets assigned to your family and will then be your first and last point of contact for any health condition.

In India, you can go to any doctor, be it a physician, orthopaedist, paediatrician, neurologist or a cardiac surgeon. The choice is yours. But in Canada, you cannot go to any doctor. Family doctors treat all generic illnesses. If they feel you need to see a specialist, they refer you to one. You can only book an appointment with a specialist after you have been referred. Specialists will not entertain you if you have not been referred.

Moreover, even if you have been referred, seeing a specialist involves a waiting period of approximately two months. We made the mistake of thinking that, if referred, we would be approached by a specialist or lab, but that's not the case. You have to explicitly make an appointment.

How to Get a Family Doctor

There are websites with lists of clinics that are accepting new patients. You need to go to such a clinic and fill a registration form. You may have to wait for a doctor to be assigned to you. Even after you register, it may take up to four or five months, so keep looking for other clinics. Often, you will see clinics with notices that say 'Accepting New Patients'. So keep talking to the people around you. Tell them you are looking for a family doctor. They may have information that will help you. This happened to us. We were checking with all the people we knew, and one of our friends mentioned a clinic that was accepting patients. We immediately called the clinic. Fortunately, there were multiple doctors accepting patients. We randomly picked one and booked our 'meet and greet' appointment.

At the meet and greet, the doctor noted our family medical history and assigned us blood tests for certain conditions. Please note that you don't need to pay anything for blood tests or lab work.

Usually, any test recommended by the doctor will need to be booked at the same clinic. Only in certain cases will the clinic contact you to make an appointment. This depends on the type of test you need. For example, if you need a brain scan, the hospital will call to confirm your appointment, whereas for a blood test or an ENT appointment, you will have to call the lab or clinic.

In India, when you go to see a doctor, there is generally a receptionist whom you pay, after which you wait in the lobby for your turn and then proceed to the doctor's cabin to see the doctor. In Canada, you are moved from the waiting area to a room where the doctor comes to see you. The doctor may take anywhere between five and forty minutes to come. Everything is done online. You don't get a physical consultation paper or prescription. The doctor enters everything online and will even ask you which pharmacy you would like to fetch your medicine from. Your prescription will be sent to the pharmacy you choose.

Then you need to go to that pharmacy and ask for your medicines. The pharmacists will look up your details and take time to prepare your medicines.

Yes, they prepare your medicines. They don't hand over medicines in their original packaging. Rather, you get bottles labelled with the dosage, probable side effects, refill information, names of the medicine and the doctor, etc. Sometimes, this preparation may take more than an hour if multiple people are in the queue.

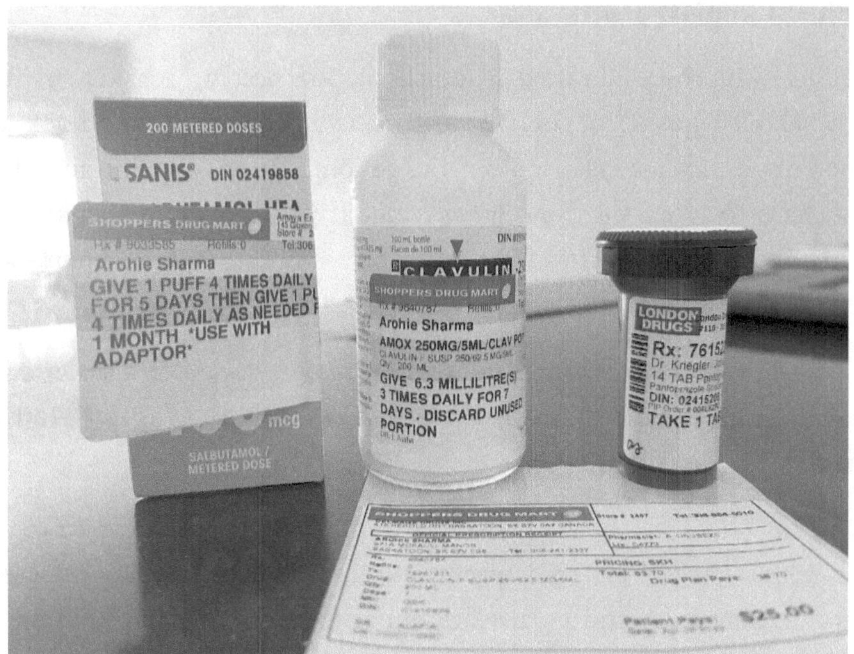

The prescription is valid only once. You cannot take more of the medicine unless it is prescribed again by a doctor. If a medicine is prescribed for, say, three months, the store might give you enough medicine for a month and mention two refills on the bottle. That means you can refill the bottle twice without seeing the doctor again.

Whenever you want to see your family doctor, you will need to make an appointment, which you may get only two or three weeks later. Simply booking the appointment may require you to wait for hours on the phone, so it's better to go to the clinic to save time. If you don't want to wait for two weeks, then each doctor has walk-in days on which they see patients as they walk in. You may choose to do so, but note that, even on those days, the waiting period may be roughly two hours or so. It's generally a good idea to get yourself enqueued and come back around the time of your appointment. There is usually a rough waiting time displayed at the reception. If there isn't, you can ask the receptionist about it.

School Registration

To get your child admitted in a school, you need to register on the city school registration site. To do that, you need to call and book an appointment. It may take a month to get one. On the appointment day, you have to go to the Newcomer Student Centre, where a small test will be conducted to assess your child's communication skills. Then your child will be assigned a class according to their age.

Saskatoon Newcomer Student Centre → https://www.saskatoon publicschools.ca/registration/noncanadian/NSC/Pages/default. aspx

The school is assigned according to the neighbourhood you live in. An admission form is printed out and handed over to you. You need to take that form and go to the school to get your child registered, which hardly takes any time. The school will ask your child to join on a particular date.

If you shift to a different neighbourhood before your child can actually start going to the assigned school, you will first need to use an online school locator to see which school your child is eligible for. Then you will need to go to that school and tell them that you submitted your child's admission form to the school that had earlier been assigned to you but have now moved to a new neighbourhood. You won't face any problems. It will take just a few minutes to enrol the child.

You may also have a school visit scheduled, during which they will let you check out the school and meet the principal.

Saskatoon Public Schools
Inspiring Learning

Elementary Registration Form 2022 – 2023
Select School

☐ English ☐ Cree Program ☐ Michif Program ☐ French Immersion

Cree Language & Cultural Program at wahkohtowin School. Michif Early Learning Program at Westmount School (PreK & K only). French Immersion available at Alvin Buckwold, College Park, Dundonald, Forest Grove, Henry Kelsey, Lakeview, River Heights, Silverspring and Victoria

Students who are not Canadian citizens must contact the Newcomer Student Centre, 310 – 21ˢᵗ Street East, (306) 683-8400

STUDENT INFORMATION

Students Legal name	Birthdate	Gender
Last Name	MMM DD YYYY	☐ Male ☐ Unspecified ☑ Female
First Name	Languages First Language Hindi	
	Second Language English	
Middle Name	Has student ever been registered with Saskatoon Public Schools? ☐ Yes ☑ No	
Usual or Called Name *(If different from First Name)*	Previous School Attended	Previous School's Location India

Registering for Grade ☑ PK ☐ K Grade ☐ 1 ☐ 2 ☐ 3 ☐ 4 ☐ 5 ☐ 6 ☐ 7 ☐ 8

First Nations, Inuit and Métis (voluntary self-declaration)

☐ First Nations Status ☐ First Nations Non-Status ☐ Inuit ☐ Métis

Reserve Name:

Citizenship | Is the named student a Canadian citizen? ☐ Yes ☑ No If No, Citizenship: India

If Not a Canadian citizen contact Newcomer Student Centre Country of Birth: India

NEWCOMER STUDENT CENTRE USE ONLY | Last Country Student Attended School: India

Proof of legal status must be provided in order to register (A copy will be placed in the student's cumulative folder.)

☑ Permanent Resident ☐ Refugee Category ☐ Parent Work Permit Exp mm/dd/yyyy
☐ Study Permit (International Student Program) ☐ Parent Study Permit Exp mm/dd/yyyy

Signature of School official Verifying document

OFFICE USE ONLY How was the students name and birthdate verified?

☐ Birth Certificate ☐ Passport ☐ Status Card
☑ Immigration Papers / Permanent Resident Card Other (Name Official Document)

Signature of School official Verifying document

STUDENT'S RESIDENCE / STUDENT'S CONTACT INFORMATION

STUDENT'S RESIDENCE	STUDENT'S CONTACT INFORMATION
House Number Apt# (if applicable)	Home Phone
Street	Email
City Saskatoon	Cell Phone
Province SK Postal Code S7M 5M8	Student Resides with ☑ Two Parents ☐ Mother ☐ Father ☐ Joint Custody ☐ Relative ☐ Guardian

---

EMERGENCY / MEDICAL INFORMATION

Who should be contacted first in the case of school closure or an emergency? (i.e. Mother, Father, Guardian)

1.
2.
3. Other Emergency Contact Name: Phone
4. Other Emergency Contact Name: Phone

Life Threatening Medical Condition(s) that requires regular medication or requires emergency medication that the school should be aware of.

Other Medical Condition(s) that the school should be aware of.

Child Care	
Name	Phone

GUARDIANSHIP RIGHTS, CUSTODY, OR ACCESS RIGHTS | Indicate if such document(s) exist: ☐ Yes ☐ No

Type of Legal Document: ☐ Access and/or Custody ☐ Parenting ☐ Guardianship ☐ Protection ☐ Other

Copy in Student Record: ☐ Yes ☐ No   Document Expiry Date (if applicable)

OFFICE USE ONLY (NOTES):

First parent/Guardian	☑ Father ☐ Mother ☐ Step father ☐ Step Mother ☐ Legal Guardian ☐ Other
Last Name	Address if different from Student
First Name	House/Apt #
Title ☑ Mr. ☐ Mrs. ☐ Ms. ☐ Miss ☐ Dr.	Street
☑ Married ☐ Single ☐ Separated ☐ Divorced ☐ Other	City
Phone	Province / Postal Code
Email ____@gmail.com	Employer
Cell	Employer Phone ( )

Second parent/Guardian	☐ Father ☑ Mother ☐ Step father ☐ Step Mother ☐ Legal Guardian ☐ Other
Last Name	Address if different from Student
First Name	House/Apt #
Title ☐ Mr. ☑ Mrs. ☐ Ms. ☐ Miss ☐ Dr.	Street
☑ Married ☐ Single ☐ Separated ☐ Divorced ☐ Other	City
Phone	Province / Postal Code
Email	Employer
Cell	Employer Phone

Third parent/Guardian	☐ Father ☐ Mother ☐ Step father ☐ Step Mother ☐ Legal Guardian ☐ Other
Last Name	Address if different from Student
First Name	House/Apt #
Title ☐ Mr. ☐ Mrs. ☐ Ms. ☐ Miss ☐ Dr.	Street
☐ Married ☐ Single ☐ Separated ☐ Divorced ☐ Other	City
Phone ( )	Province / Postal Code
Email	Employer
Cell ( )	Employer Phone ( )

Fourth parent/Guardian	☐ Father ☐ Mother ☐ Step father ☐ Step Mother ☐ Legal Guardian ☐ Other
Last Name	Address if different from Student
First Name	House/Apt #
Title ☐ Mr. ☐ Mrs. ☐ Ms. ☐ Miss ☐ Dr.	Street
☐ Married ☐ Single ☐ Separated ☐ Divorced ☐ Other	City
Phone ( )	Province / Postal Code
Email	Employer
Cell ( )	Employer Phone ( )

Please list siblings living in the same home

Siblings Full Name	Birthdate (MMM-DD-YYYY)	Current School	Grade

Employees of Saskatoon Public Schools may use the information collected on this form to help provide appropriate educational programming and support for the student.

Demographic information is shared with Saskatchewan Ministry of Education to support the Student Data System. How this information is accessed, used, or disclosed is protected under the **Freedom of Information and Protection of Privacy Act** *and the* **Local Authority Freedom of Information and Protection of Privacy Act.**

Note: Your child is not officially registered until legal documentation is brought directly to the school and verified by school personnel.

Declaration

I, the undersigned, hereby represent that I have the legal authority to register the child. I declare the information that I have provided on this form is complete and accurate. *I will notify the school of any changes to the information on this form.*

Date	Signature of Parent / Custodial Parent / Legal Guardian
June 21, 2022	

The amazing part is that you don't need to pay the school a fee. Even the transport is completely free.

Newcomer Help Centres

Dealing with all the new processes and systems in a new country can be overwhelming for immigrants, especially if they have to do everything on their own, so it is always good if someone can help with all the nitty-gritties.

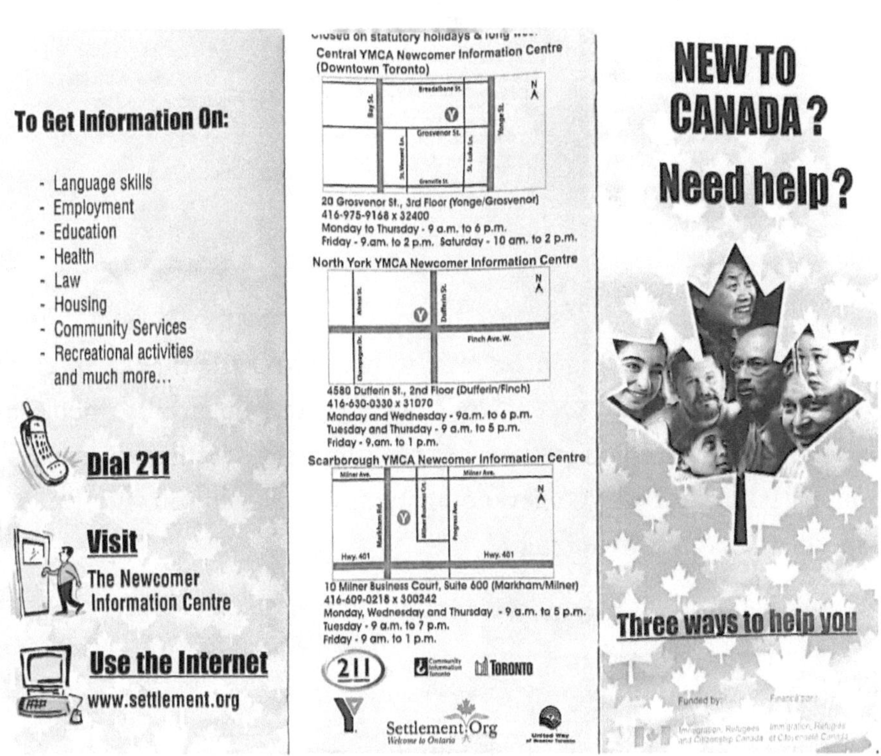

In Canada, several agencies exist to help you settle in, like Internal Women of Saskatoon, Open Door Society, etc. You need to book an appointment with them so that they can carve out a settlement plan for you in detail. They assign relevant organisations to help you with various aspects of your life, including:

- English improvement
- Housing needs
- Benefits
- Employment and career training
- Health card
- Social support and community support. This is very useful for those who have a limited skill set or understanding of how things work in Canada and feel incapable of doing everything on their own. I took the help of Open Door Society while applying for our PR cards.

Sample Settlement Plan

IWS

SETTLEMENT ACTION PLAN				
Client Name:	*Shuchita SINGH*	**Date of NAARS/Triage Appointment:**	MM 06	DD 07	Year 2022
Internal ID #:	5813	**IWS Staff:**		

Summary of my **Goals**:	**SHORT:** I want to improve my English language to improve it further if needed. I want the information to enroll in M.BA program. I want information about registering with a family doctor. I want information about the recreational activities to join and to connect with the community. I want information about summer programs for my children. I want information about the French language. I want information about the family doctor. I want to search for a job a little later. I want to get assistance to apply for jobs. I want information about child tax benefits. I want to apply for a health card. I want the information to apply for Driver's license. I want information about tax returns. **MID:** I want to complete the M.BA course to upgrade my education. I want to get stable employment. **LONG:**	Summary of my **Needs**:	I need to contact the organization to attend English classes if needed to improve it further. I need to contact organizations and need to attend employment training programs to get assistance to apply for the jobs. I need to contact the doctor's clinic and register with a family doctor. I need to contact the community center and enroll myself in recreational activities and summer programs for my children. I need to contact SGI to apply for my driving license. I need to check the details for child tax benefits and need to apply for child tax benefits for my children. I need to contact e-health and register for a health card. I need to check the details of tax returns and when needed to apply I will apply for my tax returns. I need to check the details and will enroll for the French language. I need to study and complete the M.BA course to upgrade my education. I need to apply for multiple job openings in the applied Engineering/ M.BA field to get a stable job.

Version 3.0 Last Updated June 18, 2021
International Women of Saskatoon (IWS) Inc.
www.iwssaskatoon.org

1

IWS

	I want to become a Canadian citizen. I want to settle down in Canada and would like to have a balanced life. I want to pursue a career in the M.BA field.		I need to apply for multiple jobs to get a permanent full-time job in the applied Engineering/ M.BA field. I need to apply for my citizenship once I will be eligible for the same.
Summary of my **Assets & Strengths:** (skills, knowledge, experience, supports)	I have 2 Master's degrees. I have vast foreign work experience. I have a full-time job. I have an excellent relationship with my spouse and with my children. I feel safe and happy in Saskatoon. I am determined to accomplish my goal. I have very good communication skills. I am keen to learn new skills. I have a positive outlook on life.	Summary of my **Values & Interests**:	I value education. I value my family and social life. I value balanced life. I value Independence. I like to like to join recreational activities. I like traveling/seeing the world

ACTIONS AND REFERRALS			
PRIORITY In order of urgency	**ACTIONS I WILL TAKE:** To achieve my goals and address my needs	**RELEVANT NAARS THEME**	**SERVICE PROVIDER** **PROGRAM/SERVICE** **CONTACT INFORMATION FOR REGISTRATION** (address, phone number, email, website)	**TIMELINE** A. SHORT TERM 3-6 months B. MIDTER MERM 7m-2years C. LONG TERM 2+ years

Version 3.0 Last Updated June 18, 2021
International Women of Saskatoon (IWS) Inc.
www.iwssaskatoon.org

2

54

#				
1.	I will contact the **Saskatoon Open Door Society (SODS)** so that I can get support with my settlement needs. I will contact SODS if I need assistance with the searching house, child tax benefits, health card etc.	IMMEDIATE NEEDS/ LIFE SKILLS	**Saskatoon Open Door Society (SODS)** **Zone Agency Case Coordination Services** 100-129 3rd Ave N, Saskatoon, SK S7K 2H4 Tel. 306-653-4464 https://www.sods.sk.ca/welcoming/get-settled	SHORT TERM
2.	I will check the details for the child tax benefits and I will apply for the same for my children.	CHILDREN	*Saskatchewan* **Child Care Subsidy** https://www.saskatchewan.ca/residents/family-and-social-support/child-care/paying-for-child-care **List of childcare centres in your community:** (this lists all the daycares so that you can remain free of any conflict of interest)https://www.saskatchewan.ca/residents/family-and-social-support/child-care/find-a-child-care-provider-in-my-community **Childcare Providers** https://www.saskatchewan.ca/residents/family-and-social-support/child-care/find-a-child-care-provider-in-my-community	SHORT TERM
3.	I will check for safe and affordable housing.	HOUSING	**Saskatoon Housing Authority** http://saskatoonhousingauthority.com/accessible-housing/ **QUINT**	SHORT TERM

Version 3.0 Last Updated June 18, 2021
International Women of Saskatoon (IWS) Inc.
www.iwssaskatoon.org

3

IWS

	I will check the details if I am eligible for a subsidy and will apply for a subsidy for housing.		https://quintsaskatoon.ca/programs/apply-rental-housing/ **Government of Saskatchewan** https://www.saskatchewan.ca/residents/housing-and-renting/renting-and-leasing/rental-housing-for-people-with-low-incomes	
4.	I will contact the career services to enroll in the M.BA programs.	FORMAL EDUCATION	**University of Saskatchewan** Career planning / **Career Services** University of Saskatchewan G50 Lower Marquis Hall 97 Campus Drive Saskatoon SK S7N 4L3 Monday–Friday 8:30-4:30 https://students.usask.ca/jobs/careers.ph **University of Saskatchewan** Business Administration Master of Business Administration (M.B.A.) Contact: Edwards Graduate Programs Room 241 Edwards School of Business 25 Campus Drive University of Saskatchewan Saskatoon, SK S7N 5A7 Admissions Officer Chandra Kretzer Email: mba@edwards.usask.ca https://programs.usask.ca/grad-studies/business-administration/index.php	SHORT TERM

Version 3.0 Last Updated June 18, 2021
International Women of Saskatoon (IWS) Inc.
www.iwssaskatoon.org

#				
5.	I will check the school available for my elder child and pre-school in my area for my younger child.	CHILDREN	**Government of Saskatchewan** https://www.saskatchewan.ca/residents/education-and-learning/prek-12-education-early-learning-and-schools/prekindergarten	SHORT TERM
6.	I will participate in employment training programs when I need to search for another job so that I can get help with my job search.	EMPLOYMENT AND CAREER TRAINING	**Saskatchewan Intercultural Association (SIA)** Employment Counselling one-o-one Tel. 306-978-1818 https://saskintercultural.org/employment-programs/employment-counselling-services-program-ecs/ **Saskatchewan Intercultural Association (SIA)** *Mentorship Program* 601b 1st Ave N, Saskatoon, SK S7K 1X7 Tel. 306-978-1818 https://www.saskintercultural.org/programs/employment/mentorship-program **Saskatchewan Intercultural Association (SIA)** *CareerNet* 601b 1st Ave N, Saskatoon, SK S7K 1X7 Tel. 306-978-1818 https://saskintercultural.org/employment-programs/careernet-program/ **Saskatchewan Intercultural Association (SIA)** Bridging to Employment is SIA's newest employment program CONTACT US T (306) 978-1818 F (306) 978 -1411	SHORT TERM TO MIDTERM

Version 3.0 Last Updated June 18, 2021
International Women of Saskatoon (IWS) Inc.
www.iwssaskatoon.org

5

Address:
601B 1st Avenue North, Saskatoon, S7K 1X7
https://saskintercultural.org/employment-programs/bridging-to-employment-program/#:~:text=Bridging%20to%20Emp

Saskatoon Open Door Society (SODS)
Employment Program services
100-129 3rd Ave N, Saskatoon, SK S7K 2H4
Tel. 306-653-4464
https://www.sods.sk.ca/

Trades and Skills Center
450 Avenue W North, Saskatoon SK, S7L 1C1
Call: 306.385.3500
Email: stsc@saskatoontradesandskills.ca
https://www.saskatoontradesandskills.ca/

Ministry of Immigration and Career Training
Labour Market Services Office
225 - 1st Avenue North
Saskatoon, SK
+1-833-613-0485
https://www.saskatchewan.ca/residents/jobs-working-and-training/labour-market-services#contact-us

YWCA Saskatoon
https://ywcasaskatoon.com/employment-learning/
Job Finding Club (held every month)
Contact the Facilitator at 306-986-2876

Achev

Version 3.0 Last Updated June 18, 2021
International Women of Saskatoon (IWS) Inc.
www.iwssaskatoon.org

Career Counselling
One-on-one Career Counselling
1-888-558-0282
Email. info@careerloans.ca
https://careerloans.ca/how-it-works

Canadian Online Job Posting
Canadian Online Job Posting Dashboard - LMIC-CIMT (lmic-cimt.ca)
The Canadian Online Job Posting Dashboard is an interactive tool allowing users to explore timely detailed labour market information related to online job postings by occupation, geography, time period and work requirements.

SaskJobs – Career Services
Toll-free Number → 1-833-613-0485
Email address → careerservices@gov.sk.ca
https://www.saskatchewan.ca/residents/jobs-working-and-training/saskjobs-career-services

Trades and Skills Center
450 Avenue W North, Saskatoon SK, S7L 1C1
Call: 306.385.3500
Email: stsc@saskatoontradesandskills.ca
https://www.saskatoontradesandskills.ca/

Express Employment Professionals
236 3 Ave S, Saskatoon, SK S7K 1L9
Phone: (306) 664-1441
expresspros.com

IWS

			Randstad Canada 310 Wall St, Saskatoon, SK S7K 1N7 Phone: (306) 202-8851 https://www.randstad.ca/job-seeker/locations/find-a-job-in-saskatoon-saskatchewan_3219/ **Radius Community Centre for Education and Employment Training** https://radiuscentre.com/ **Quint Development** 1120 20th St W suite 101, Saskatoon, SK S7M 0Y8 Tel. 306-978-4041 https://quintsaskatoon.ca/programs/core-neighbourhoods-at-work/find-a-job/	
7.	I will check the website and will check to apply for a health card and for a family doctor available in my area so that I can enroll myself and my family with a family doctor.	PERSONAL ANF FAMILY HEALTH AND WELL-BEING	**To apply for a health card** **eHealth Saskatchewan** https://www.ehealthsask.ca/residents/health-cards/Pages/Apply-for-a-Health-Card.aspx **Saskatchewan Health Authority** https://www.saskatoonhealthregion.ca/patients/Pages/Doctors-Taking-Patients.aspx **Find the list of doctors under** Doctors Accepting New Patients **(PDF)** **Why you need a family doctor** https://albertafindadoctor.ca/pages/why-you-need-a-family-doctor **Saskatchewan Health Authority** **Walk-in Clinics**	SHORT TERM

Version 3.0 Last Updated June 18, 2021
International Women of Saskatoon (IWS) Inc.
www.iwssaskatoon.org

8

			https://www.saskatoonhealthregion.ca/locations_services/locations/Pages/Walk-in-Clinics.aspx	
8.	I will check the website for Volunteer opportunities to get Canadian work experience in my field.	EMPLOYMENT AND CAREER TRAINING	**University of Saskatchewan** Volunteer Opportunities "Volunteerism and the sense of compassion that community services help develop are fundamental to achieving sustainability." - AASHE Contact Web: http://www.ecofriendlysask.ca Email: ecofriendlysask@gmail.com https://sustainability.usask.ca/get-involved/volunteer-opportunities.php **Volunteer Connector** https://www.volunteerconnector.org/ **United Way Volunteer Database** https://unitedwaysaskatoon.ca/volunteer-database/	SHORT TERM
9.	I will check the details and will enroll in French language classes.	LANGUAGE	**College Mathieu** Contact Mr. Mamady Camara, Provincial Continuing Education Coordinator: education.saskatoon@collegemathieu.sk.ca Tel : 306 384 2722 https://www.collegemathieu.sk.ca/languages-classes/french-courses-for-immigrants-clic-cours-de-langue-pour-les-immigrants-au-canada	MID TERM
10.	I will check the website to apply for a driving license and I will attend the programs which will help me to get the license.	IMMEDIATE NEEDS/ LIFE SKILLS	**Quint** *Driver Education Program* (*Free Services*) 101 – 1120 20th Street West	SHORT TERM

IWS

			Saskatoon, SK, S7M 0Y8 Tel. 306-978-4041 ext. 243 https://quintsaskatoon.ca/programs/core-neighbourhoods-at-work/find-a-job/ Please note that you must have held your Class 7 learner's license for 7 months to be eligible for this program. Also, note that there might be a long waiting list. Contact QUINT to find out how long the wait time is. **SGI** https://www.sgi.sk.ca/ 623 2nd Ave N, Saskatoon, SK S7K 0H3 Tel. 306-683-2100 **Saskatoon Open Door Society (SODS)** *SGI Drivers' Education* 100-129 3rd Ave N, Saskatoon, SK S7K 2H4 306-653-4464 https://www.sods.sk.ca/	
11.	I will check the websites of the city of Saskatoon to join the recreational activities.	SOCIAL SUPPORT AND COMMUNITY CONNECTIONS	**City of Saskatoon Leisure Centres** **Leisure Guide** https://www.saskatoon.ca/parks-recreation-attractions/recreational-activities-fitness/leisure-guide _Low or no cost opportunities_ https://www.saskatoon.ca/parks-recreation-attractions/recreational-programs-activities/low-cost-no-cost-opportunities **Leisure Centres Admission Rates and Options**	Short term

10

Version 3.0 Last Updated June 18, 2021
International Women of Saskatoon (IWS) Inc.
www.iwssaskatoon.org

![IWS]

#	Action	Category	Resources	Term
			https://www.saskatoon.ca/parks-recreation-attractions/recreational-facilities-sportsfields/leisure-centres/leisure-centre-admission-rates-options **City of Saskatoon Community Associations** https://www.saskatoon.ca/all-community-association-programs	
12.	I will check the details for student loans if I need to apply for the same to upgrade my education.	FORMAL EDUCATION	**Saskatchewan Student Grants** https://www.saskatchewan.ca/residents/education-and-learning/scholarships-bursaries-grants/grants-and-bursaries/canada-and-saskatchewan-student-grants#full-time-students-from-middle-income-families **Student Loans** https://www.saskatchewan.ca/residents/education-and-learning/student-loans	SHORT TERM
13.	I will check the summer programs for the children and will contact organizations and centers to enroll my children so that children can join summer programs.	CHILDREN	**Saskatchewan Intercultural Association (SIA)** *ConnectED Summer* https://saskintercultural.org/youth-programs/connected-summer/ Apply here: https://saskintercultural.org/youth-program-application/ 601b 1st Ave N, Saskatoon, SK S7K 1X7 Tel. 306-978-1818 Saskatoon Open door Society (choose the program) Programs for Youth and Students Helping Youth Get More Engaged After-School Programs Youth Empowerment Workshops	

Version 3.0 Last Updated June 18, 2021
International Women of Saskatoon (IWS) Inc.
www.iwssaskatoon.org

11

IWS

Youth Sports Training and Activities
SSWIS Summer Camps
Summer Activities for Youth
Youth Leadership Programs
SODS 3rd Ave Location
100 - 129 3rd Ave N.
Saskatoon, SK
S7K 2H4
P. 306-653-4464 | F. 306-653-7159
https://www.sods.sk.ca/connecting/programs-for-youth-and-students

YMCA
YOUTH PROGRAMS
Financial Assistance
https://ymcasaskatoon.org/events
(fees apply)

Family Fun Saskatoon
FREE Soccer in Your Neighborhood this Summer with Saskatoon Youth Soccer
https://www.familyfuncanada.com/saskatoon/kids-in-the-park/
Website: saskatoonyouthsoccer.ca/

City of Saskatoon
Summer Activities
https://www.saskatoon.ca/parks-recreation-attractions/recreational-programs-activities/summer-saskatoon-find-your-fun

City of Saskatoon

Version 3.0 Last Updated June 18, 2021
International Women of Saskatoon (IWS) Inc.
www.iwssaskatoon.org

IWS

| | | Outdoor Pools
https://www.saskatoon.ca/parks-recreation-attractions/recreational-facilities-sportsfields/outdoor-pools-paddling-pools-spray-pads | |

INFORMATIONAL RESOURCES / WEBSITES (TO READ)		
NAME / Title of Resource	NAARS Theme	Web URL / Attachment
I will download the Welcome to Saskatchewan APP so that I can have continuous access to important information relating to settlements in Saskatchewan and Canada in general.	IMMEDIATE NEEDS & LIFE SKILLS	**International Women of Saskatoon** *Download the Welcome to Saskatchewan APP* https://iwssaskatoon.org/welcome-to-saskatchewan/ Please note that this APP features; • A to-do list for newcomers • Where to find resources in the community • And other important information for newcomers.
I will see the details for hospitals in the city for any health emergency.	PERSONAL AND FAMILY HEALTH AND WELLBEING	Hospital **Royal University Hospital** 103 Hospital Drive, Saskatoon 1-306-655-1000 | Get Directions Hospital **Saskatoon City Hospital** 701 Queen Street, Saskatoon 306-655-8000 | Get Directions **St. Paul's Hospital** 20th Street West, Saskatoon, SK, Canada **Find a Hospital**

Version 3.0 Last Updated June 18, 2021
International Women of Saskatoon (IWS) Inc.
www.iwssaskatoon.org

13

IWS

		https://www.saskatchewan.ca/residents/health/emergency-medical-services/find-a-hospital Before a health Card, one has to pay the doctor fees depending on the family doctor/walk-in clinic fees. Can apply/contact for reimbursement for the paid fees, once get the health card to : Health Medical Services Contact number: 306-787-3475 or can check with the health region. The same applies to emergency hospital visits, need to pay the hospital bills and then can apply for reimbursement once get a health card, the amount depends on the individual case and how much one can get back.
I will check the websites for the community programs and festivals so that I can connect with the community.	SOCIAL SUPPORT AND COMMUNITY CONNECTIONS	**folkfest** **Watch Culture Connect Folkfest 2021 –** **A Virtual Experience!** **Plans are underway for Saskatoon Folkfest 2022 – August 18,19, & 20. Follow us on social media to keep up to date!** **Contact Us** **Phone: (306) 931-0100** **Email:saskatoonfolkfest@gmail.com** https://saskatoonfolkfest.com/ **India-Canada Cultural Association** http://www.iccasaskatoon.ca/ **Hindu Society of Saskatoon** 107 La Ronge Rd, Saskatoon, SK S7K 5T3 Phone (306) 933-4041 https://www.slntemple.ca/ **Shree Hindu Swaminarayan Temple (ISSO)** **Address: 103 Marquis Ct #110, Saskatoon, SK S7P 0A3**

IWS

		(306) 341-3291 https://www.swaminarayan.info/temples/canada/shree-swaminarayan-hindu-temple-saskatoon **BAPS Shri Swaminarayan Mandir, Saskatoon** Address: 160 Cartwright St E, Saskatoon, SK S7T 1B1 (306) 801-2277 https://www.baps.org/saskatoon
I will check the website for Canadian tax information o that I can apply my tax returns when needed.	BUDGETING/FINANCE	**Government of Canada** **Income tax information:** https://www.canada.ca/en/revenue-agency/services/tax/individuals/educational-programs/learning-about-taxes/learning-material.html
I will contact the **Professional Engineers group of Saskatchewan to connect with the professionals.**	FORMAL EDUCATION	**Association of Professional Engineers & Geoscientists of Saskatchewan** https://www.apegs.ca/Portal/Pages/International-Engineering-Graduates 300 4581 Parliament Avenue Regina, SK, S4W 0G3 Tel. 306 525-9547 **International graduate inquiries:** questions-academicreview@apegs.ca
To buy a used car -	IMMEDIATE NEEDS	**How to buy new and used vehicles** https://www.sgi.sk.ca/new-and-used-vehicles
I will enroll in the women's programs to learn new skills and connect with the community.	SOCIAL SUPPORT AND COMMUNITY CONNECTIONS	**International Women of Saskatoon (IWS)** Just4Women 301-336 5th Avenue North Saskatoon, SK . S7K 2P4 Tel: 306-978-6611 Fax: 306-978-6614 Email: info@iwssaskatoon.org https://iwssaskatoon.org/just4women-3/

IWS

For more information about your Settlement Action Plan, please contact your NAARS Case Worker or Triage Counsellor:

Name	Position/Title	Phone Number	Email
	NAARS Case Worker	Direct line: 306-651-1480 Main Office: 306-978-6611	naars2.saskatoon@iwssaskatoon.org

Client Signature: ________________________________   Date: (MM/DD/YYYY) ____________________

16

Version 3.0 Last Updated June 18, 2021
International Women of Saskatoon (IWS) Inc.
www.iwssaskatoon.org

Social Insurance Number (SIN)

After landing, you will have to visit the nearest Services Canada office for your SIN Card. As usual, you need to call them and book an appointment before visiting their office. This process hardly takes any time. Only a few forms have to be filled, and a SIN is generated for each family member, even for kids, irrespective of age. You will get the SIN immediately as a printout, signed and stamped on the same day and at the same time.

The SIN is like the Indian PAN, but **you are not to share this number with anyone except when it is required for certain banking formalities.** This number will be sufficient for all further actions in Canada—securing a job, opening a bank account, house hunting, etc. The card will reach you in approximately three weeks.

NOTE: Remember, you don't need the SIN Card for anything. You only need the number. It is wise to visit a Services Canada office the day after you arrive.

IMPORTANT NOTE: Both the PR Card and SIN Card are federal documents, i.e. they are valid across the entire nation of Canada.

Sample SIN provided

Service Canada

Date: **Jun 01, 2022 / 01 juin 2022**

Canada

PROTECTED B / PROTÉGÉ B

SHUCHITA SINGH
1008 - 90 22ND ST E
SASKATOON SK S7K 3X6

Social Insurance Number (SIN) / Numéro d'assurance sociale (NAS):

Names on the SIN record / Noms au dossier de NAS

First Name / Prénom:
Middle Name(s) / Second(s) prénom(s):
Family Name(s) / Nom(s) de famille:

SHUCHITA

SINGH

Protect your SIN; it is confidential
Keep any document containing your SIN in a safe place.

Protégez votre NAS, il est confidentiel
Conservez tout document où l'on retrouve votre NAS dans un endroit sûr.

Use of your SIN
You are required to provide your SIN to your employer within three days after the day you receive it. Also, some programs and/or services authenticate a person's identity using data on the SIN record; ensure you are using the names as shown above.

Utilisation de votre NAS
Vous devez fournir votre NAS à votre employeur dans les trois jours suivant sa réception. Aussi, certains programmes et/ou services utilisent les données au dossier de NAS afin d'authentifier l'identité d'une personne. Assurez-vous d'utiliser les noms qui figurent ci-dessus.

If your SIN begins with the number 9
You must present a valid proof of authorization to work in Canada to your employer. Your SIN record must be updated to reflect the most recent expiry date.

Si votre NAS débute par le chiffre 9
Vous devez présenter à votre employeur une autorisation valide vous permettant de travailler au Canada. Votre dossier de NAS doit être mis à jour afin de refléter la plus récente date d'expiration.

For more information, visit our Web site:
Canada.ca/social-insurance-number

Pour plus de renseignements, consultez notre site Web :
Canada.ca/numero-assurance-sociale

PROTECTING YOUR SOCIAL INSURANCE NUMBER

Your SIN is confidential and it's important to protect it from fraudulent use.

Your Social Insurance Number (SIN) being used to commit fraud could ruin your credit rating and make it very hard to get credit in the future.

Someone might use your SIN to receive your government payments or tax refunds or to work illegally. If your SIN is used to work illegally, the Canada Revenue Agency could expect you to pay tax on income you did not receive.

How to protect your SIN

- ▶ If you have a SIN card, do not carry it in your wallet or purse—store it in a safe place.
- ▶ Never use your SIN as a piece of identification.
- ▶ Provide your SIN only when you know that it is legally required.
- ▶ Provide your SIN over the phone only if you make the call and you know it is legally required.
- ▶ Never reply to emails that ask for personal information like your SIN.
- ▶ Shred paper records with your SIN once you no longer need them—do not recycle them.
- ▶ Contact Service Canada if you change your name, if your citizenship status changes, or if information on your SIN record is incorrect or incomplete.
- ▶ Take action immediately to protect your SIN if you suspect someone is using it fraudulently. See the section: *If you suspect someone is using your SIN or have been victim of fraud* below.

Service
Canada

Examples of when you **DO NOT** have to provide your SIN:

▶ proving your identity (except for certain government programs)
▶ applying for a job
▶ applying to rent a property
▶ negotiating a lease with a landlord
▶ applying for a credit card
▶ cashing a cheque
▶ completing some banking transactions (mortgage, line of credit, loan)
▶ completing a medical questionnaire
▶ renting a car
▶ signing up for cell phone, Internet or TV services
▶ writing a will
▶ applying to a university or college

If you are asked for your SIN when it is not legally required

If your SIN is not required by law, ask why it is being requested, how it will be used, and with whom it will be shared. Explain that your SIN is not required by law and that you do not want to provide it. Offer a different proof of identity.

If the company or organization refuses to provide the product or service unless you provide your SIN, ask to speak to the person in charge. Many companies and organizations do not know about the appropriate uses of the SIN. Once they understand, they may willingly change their practices.

If you are not satisfied with the organization's response, you are entitled to file a complaint with the Office of the Privacy Commissioner of Canada. For more information on this or on laws about your privacy and the Government of Canada, call **1-800-282-1376** or visit **www.priv.gc.ca**.

If you suspect someone is using your SIN or have been victim of fraud

If you suspect that someone else is using your SIN, act quickly to help prevent personal loss and minimize the negative impact.

An indication that your SIN is being used fraudulently could be if the Canada Revenue Agency sends you a Notice of Reassessment concerning undeclared earnings. This may mean that someone has used your SIN for employment purposes or to receive other taxable income.

When to provide your SIN

▶ after being hired by your employer

▶ when completing your income tax information

▶ when opening an account from which you earn interest at a financial institution such as a bank or credit union

▶ when accessing government programs and benefits such as:
- **Canada Pension Plan** benefits
- **Quebec Pension Plan** benefits
- **Old Age Security** benefits
- **Employment Insurance** benefits
- **Registered Education Savings Plans** (RESP)
- **Registered Disability Savings Plans** (RDSP)
- **Canada Child Benefit**
- **Canada Student Loans**
- Goods and Services Tax/Harmonized Sales Tax (GST/HST) claims
- Social assistance benefits
- **Veterans' benefits and programs**
- Workers' compensation benefits
- Child support payments

The **Social Insurance Number Code of Practice**, available online at **Canada.ca/social-insurance-number**, lists the federal programs that are permitted to use the SIN.

Some businesses may ask for you for your SIN. This is strongly discouraged, but it is not illegal.

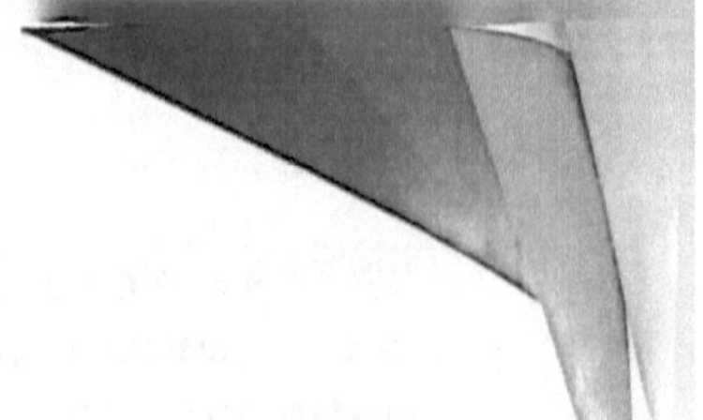

Here are some key steps to follow:

1. **File a report with the police.** Ask for the case reference number and the officer's name and telephone number. Make sure the report states your name and SIN.

2. **Report the fraud to the Canadian Anti-Fraud Centre** on their website or by calling **1-888-495-8501**.

3. **Contact Canada's two major credit bureaus** to tell them you have been a victim of identity fraud:

   Equifax Canada   **TransUnion Canada**
   1-800-465-7166   **1-800-663-9980**

   Ask each credit bureau for a copy of your credit report. (There may be a fee.) Obtain information about having a **fraud warning** be placed on your file, instructing creditors to contact you personally before opening new accounts in your name. (There may be a fee).

4. **Review both credit reports.** Look for accounts that you didn't open yourself, or creditors that have made inquiries on your credit report when you didn't ask for credit. If you see anything like this in your credit report, contact each of these creditors and tell them about the identity theft. Ask them to close any accounts you didn't open and decline any new accounts you didn't request.

5. **Review all your banking and credit card statements.** If you notice suspicious transactions, immediately contact the financial institution.

6. **Report any problems with your mail to Canada Post** — for example, if you receive opened envelopes, or do not receive your financial statements.

7. **Visit a Service Canada Centre.** You must bring proof that someone has used your SIN and the police report. You will also need to bring a valid primary identity document (for example, a birth certificate or Certificate of Canadian citizenship). A Service Canada official will help you. Your case may be referred to an investigator. Service Canada may issue a new SIN but only if there is proof that your SIN was used fraudulently.

Here's what you will need to provide to Service Canada if you suspect someone is using your SIN:

To work:

▶ a printout of a list of all the employers who issued a T4 slip for your SIN over the past three years. Call the Canada Revenue Agency at **1-800-959-8281** to ask for this printout. Check for any employers for whom you have **not** worked. Service Canada will contact them on your behalf.

▶ a clear photograph of yourself for every employer on the list for whom you did **not** work. Photographs make it easier for a Service Canada official to confirm with the employer(s) that you didn't work for them.

▶ a list of every address where you lived over the last 10 years.

To obtain credit:

▶ a copy of the credit application from the credit issuer where your **SIN** was used to obtain credit. This application must have been filled in by someone else and show **both** your name and your SIN.

▶ a letter from a creditor confirming that someone else used your **SIN** to apply for credit. This letter must include **both** your name and SIN and state that you are not responsible for any purchases made fraudulently using your information.

If you have been issued a new SIN

If Service Canada issues you a new SIN, you will need to contact all your financial institutions, creditors, pension providers and employers (most recent and current) to ask them to update your files. **Note:** Service Canada cannot correct a credit file. You must contact your financial institution(s) yourself

Getting a new SIN will not protect you from fraud or identity theft. If someone else uses your old SIN and the business does not check the person's identity with the credit bureau, credit lenders may still ask you to pay the impostor's debts. Each time, you will have to prove that you were not involved in the fraud.

For more information

For more information on how to protect yourself from fraud and identity theft, visit the following websites:

▶ **Canada's Privacy Commissioner**
   www.priv.gc.ca

▶ **Canadian Anti-Fraud Centre**
   www.antifraudcentre-centreantifraude.ca

▶ **Office of Consumer Affairs**
   www.ic.gc.ca/OCA

For more information

🖱 Click **Canada.ca/social-insurance-number**

📞 Call **1-866-274-6627**
   TTY: 1-800-926-9105
   Outside Canada: **1-506-548-7961**

Banking System

The Canadian banking system is a bit different from the Indian banking system. We'll see how in this section, starting at the very beginning.

Prominent Banks

Though most international banks operate in Canada, the three main Canadian banks are presumably the best, in terms of presence and availability (branches, ATM locations, etc.):

1. Scotia Bank
2. TD Bank
3. CIBC

Opening a Bank Account

People who are in the process of relocating to Canada usually want to transfer money from India to Canada. You can carry up to $10,000 while travelling, but what if you want to transfer more? There are multiple ways to do so, one of which is to open an account from India.

Open a bank account from India and transfer funds before landing → https://straight.scotiobank.com/newcomers.html

We opened a Scotia Bank account. When choosing a bank, you can go through what it offers and make a decision based on what interests you. Scotia Bank offered us a free locker for a year, which we utilised to keep all our gold and valuables.

When you try to open an account, remember that you need to open a current account, as 'current' is used in Canada the same way 'savings' is used in India. Opening our account took only a day or two, after which we transferred money to it. You can transfer up to $70,000, but only one transaction is allowed until the account is fully activated.

You need to activate the opened account by visiting a branch of the bank. You may make an appointment, which is the preferred way, or go directly, but you have to be punctual. You cannot follow Indian stretchable time, as everyone in Canada sticks very strictly to schedule. If a dedicated slot has been allocated to you and you reach late, you will lose valuable time, as the appointment won't be extended beyond the slot. This applies to all appointments, whether they are at salons, the doctor's, or anywhere. **So be on time for all your appointments.**

Once you reach the bank for your activation appointment, it is all very professional. Although Indian private banks look the same nowadays, Canadian banks seem more corporate. A bank executive gets assigned to you to guide you with the formalities. Our executive took us to his cabin, explained everything to us and activated our account. Our debit cards were issued the same day. We put in a request for credit cards as well. Canadian banks rely heavily on individuals' credit scores when issuing loans. Credit scores are like CIBIL in India, which banks check before giving you any kind of loan. **In Canada, however, an individual's credit score is taken more seriously, so you have to build it clean and keep it clean.** To do so, you need to have a credit card, use it and pay all your bills and your credit card payments in a timely manner. With time, your credit score builds. You can fetch your credit score for free from sites like Equifax.

Six months of being in Canada and making timely payments is sufficient to apply for any kind of loan. Be vigilant about ensuring that your credit score is not checked by too many vendors, as each enquiry affects your credit score negatively. Please note that to apply for a credit card, you need to have an address, i.e., a lease agreement needs to have been signed, as the card gets directly delivered to your mailbox. If you are living in an Airbnb, you may not be able to apply.

This was how we completed the first level of banking formalities. The executive also explained the concept of a debit form to us—it is like a letter containing your bank account details that can be used to set recurring payments.

Things You Need to Learn

There are multiple aspects of the Canadian banking system that you will need to learn about, including:

1. How to (use) Interact.
2. How to deposit a cheque.
3. How to play bills directly through apps.
4. How to open an RESP account.

Here, I will introduce you to some basic concepts.

- In Canada, it is common for people to use banking apps. An interesting facility available here is Interact, which is like Canada's Paytm, but it uses email IDs, not phone numbers, to transfer money. It does not need an explicit app because it works with your banking app. The upper limit for transactions is $3,000, and this is non-negotiable. Like in India, internet banking is common in Canada.
- Chequebooks are not free; you have to pay for them. Moreover, cheques take time to get authenticated, so, while it may reflect in your bank balance, don't go by that until at least a week later.
- The RESP account is an account you open for your kids, with a limit on the amount that can be deposited in it. The Canadian government also deposits an equal amount.
- Online transactions are common. It's completely safe to share your credit card details, even your CVV, when making payments. What's disappointing, though, is that you don't get alerted about transactions, so you have to keep checking your app.
- Although you can walk into banks at any time for any of your needs, it's always better to make an appointment. You may also be assigned a financial advisor who will help you save on your taxes.
- Banks work quickly and are easy to deal with.

Scams

Scams in Canada are a bit different from scams in India. We fell prey to one such scam. Usually, scamsters use Facebook to advertise lucrative work-from-home jobs that require no skills while offering good pay. Anyone would fall for it. Scamsters will never talk to you over calls or email. They will conduct their interviews only on the Telegraph app.

Raise your eyebrows if anyone makes you such an offer. **Always try to interact through calls and email.**

Scamsters will even send you an appointment letter with a promise of a raise if they like your performance. As a work assignment, they will ask you to mail a few people and will then ask you to attach a 'gift card' as an apology for some delay in services provided by them in the past. You may try to be smart and ask for the money to be transferred before you buy the gift cards. The scamsters will then send you a fraud cheque, stating that that's the formal way of making payments and that they cannot Interact or transfer directly to your account. The catch is that cheques take a week to get authenticated. So after you deposit the cheque and the amount gets added to your balance, you assume the cheque is authentic and you go ahead and purchase the gift cards and send them to the scamsters, who quickly encash them. You realise only a week later, when your account gets frozen and you go to the bank, that you have been scammed and have suffered a loss of whatever amount the gift cards cost you. The bank will tell you that even if you have spent the balance from a fraudulent cheque, you have to refund the bank, so you cannot outsmart the scamsters if you have already purchased and sent the gift cards.

Beware of such scams. Before signing up for anything, conduct thorough research.

Renting a House

As mentioned before, the renting process varies from one province to another. In Ontario, property dealers help you get a house, whereas in Saskatoon, we had to struggle a lot. We needed to fill in applications online just to join the queue of people seeking rentals. Whether or not you are chosen as a tenant depends entirely on the landlord, who decides based on your documentation. **You have to either have an offer letter**

or proof of your bank balance to apply for a rental. In other words, you need to prove that you can afford it. Also, you need to mention local references in your application.

Our experience gave us the feeling that dealers and homeowners are in no hurry to rent out their properties. Sometimes it takes weeks to finalise a deal; hence, you need to be quick to apply. Bookings tend to happen quite a bit in advance, so you may not get a rental immediately, in which case you either have to survive in an Airbnb or get a temporary one-month rental.

We made the mistake of first visiting the rental places and then applying, which decreased our chances of getting the places. After spending three days doing this, we understood the need to apply online first.

Rental sites:

https://www.kijiji.ca/

https://www.zumper.com/

https://www.broadstreet.ca/

https://www.bwalk.com/

https://www.hazelviewproperties.com/

It is important to read the terms and conditions of your lease agreement very carefully. Multiple terms could be completely new to you. For example, if you break a one-year lease mid-way, you may need to pay a month's rent as penalty or keep paying the rent until the owner finds a new tenant. To avoid such complications, you can also opt for a month-to-month lease in which such terms don't apply, but this comes with an extra charge, something like $50 per month, and is not always available.

Other conditions include prohibitions on putting nails in walls, cleaning costs when moving out, etc. These should be taken into consideration before making a decision, so spend a good amount of time reading each and every term of your lease agreement before signing it.

The agreement is usually printed on simple paper (not bond paper).

Sample Lease

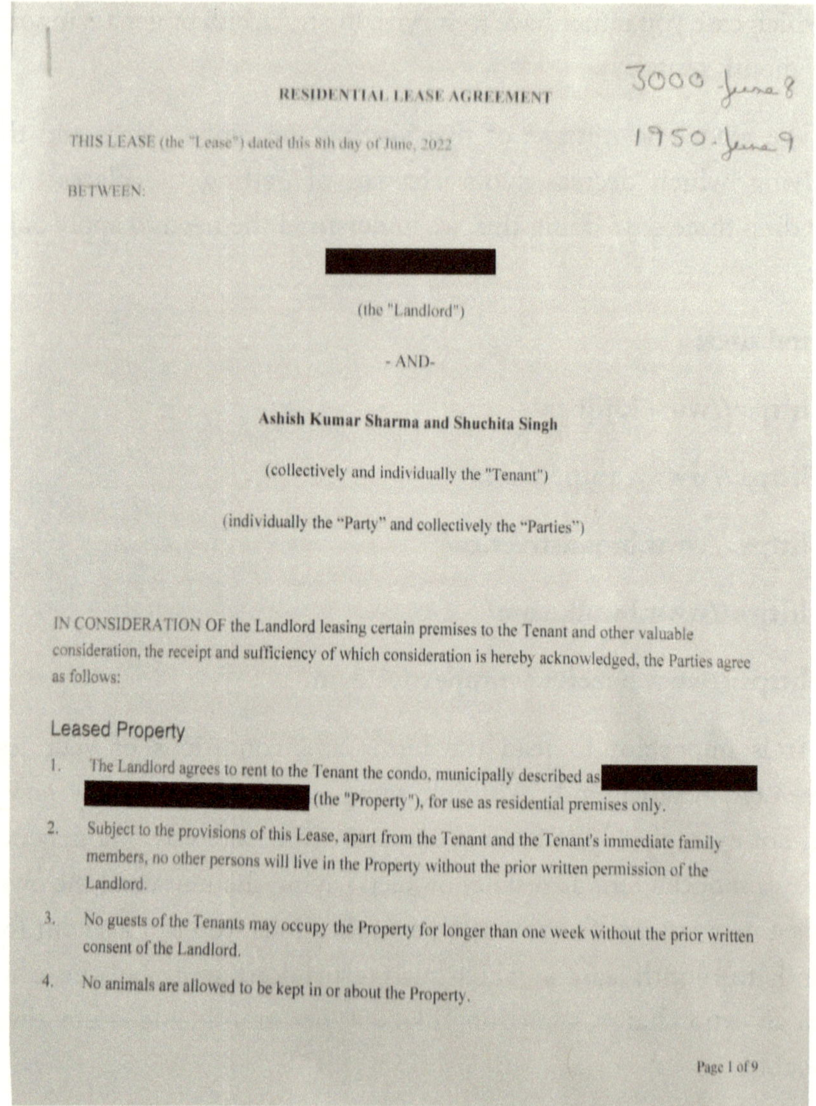

RESIDENTIAL LEASE AGREEMENT

THIS LEASE (the "Lease") dated this 8th day of June, 2022

BETWEEN:

(the "Landlord")

- AND-

Ashish Kumar Sharma and Shuchita Singh

(collectively and individually the "Tenant")

(individually the "Party" and collectively the "Parties")

IN CONSIDERATION OF the Landlord leasing certain premises to the Tenant and other valuable consideration, the receipt and sufficiency of which consideration is hereby acknowledged, the Parties agree as follows:

Leased Property

1. The Landlord agrees to rent to the Tenant the condo, municipally described as ▮▮▮▮▮▮ (the "Property"), for use as residential premises only.

2. Subject to the provisions of this Lease, apart from the Tenant and the Tenant's immediate family members, no other persons will live in the Property without the prior written permission of the Landlord.

3. No guests of the Tenants may occupy the Property for longer than one week without the prior written consent of the Landlord.

4. No animals are allowed to be kept in or about the Property.

Page 1 of 9

5. Subject to the provisions of this Lease, the Tenant is entitled to the exclusive use of the following parking on or about the Property: 174.

6. The Tenant and members of the Tenant's household will not smoke anywhere in the Property nor permit any guests or visitors to smoke in the Property.

7. The Tenant and members of the Tenant's household will not vape anywhere in the Property nor permit any guests or visitors to vape in the Property.

Term

8. The term of the Lease commences at 12:00 noon on June 8, 2022, and ends at 12:00 noon on May 31, 2023.

9. Any notice to terminate this tenancy must comply with the applicable legislation of the Province of Saskatchewan (the "Act").

Rent

10. Subject to the provisions of this Lease, the rent for the Property is $2,850.00 per month (the "Rent").

11. The Tenant will pay the Rent on or before the first (1st) day of each and every month of the term of this Lease to the Landlord at ███████████████████████ or at such other place as the Landlord may later designate by Pre Authorized.

12. The Landlord may increase the Rent for the Property upon providing to the Tenant such notice as required by the Act.

13. The Tenant will be charged an additional amount of $50.00 per infraction for any Rent that is received after the greater of 1 day after the due date and any mandatory grace period required under the Act, if any.

Security Deposit

14. On execution of this Lease, the Tenant will pay the Landlord a security deposit of $2,850.00 (the "Security Deposit").

15. During the term of this Lease or after its termination, the Landlord may charge the Tenant or make deductions from the Security Deposit for any or all of the following:

     a. repair of walls due to plugs, large nails or any unreasonable number of holes in the walls including the repainting of such damaged walls;

b. repainting required to repair the results of any other improper use or excessive damage by the Tenant;

c. unplugging toilets, sinks and drains;

d. replacing damaged or missing doors, windows, screens, mirrors or light fixtures;

e. repairing cuts, burns, or water damage to linoleum, rugs, and other areas;

f. any other repairs or cleaning due to any damage beyond normal wear and tear caused or permitted by the Tenant or by any person whom the Tenant is responsible for;

g. the cost of extermination where the Tenant or the Tenant's guests have brought or allowed insects into the Property or building;

h. repairs and replacement required where windows are left open which have caused plumbing to freeze, or rain or water damage to floors or walls;

i. replacement of locks and/or lost keys to the Property and any administrative fees associated with the replacement as a result of the Tenant's misplacement of the keys; and

j. any other purpose allowed under this Lease or the Act.

For the purpose of this clause, the Landlord may charge the Tenant for professional cleaning and repairs if the Tenant has not made alternate arrangements with the Landlord.

16. The Tenant may not use the Security Deposit as payment for the Rent.

17. The Landlord will return the Security Deposit at the end of this tenancy, less such deductions as provided in this Lease but no deduction will be made for damage due to reasonable wear and tear nor for any deduction prohibited by the Act.

18. Within the time period required by the Act and after the termination of this tenancy, the Landlord will deliver or mail the Security Deposit less any proper deductions or with further demand for payment to: ____, or at such other place as the Tenant may advise.

Inspections

19. The Parties will complete, sign and date an inspection report at the beginning and at the end of this tenancy.

20. At all reasonable times during the term of this Lease and any renewal of this Lease, the Landlord and its agents may enter the Property to make inspections or repairs, or to show the Property to

prospective tenants or purchasers in compliance with the Act.

Renewal of Lease

21. Upon giving written notice no later than 60 days before the expiration of the term of this Lease, the Tenant may renew this Lease for an additional term. All terms of the renewed lease will be the same except for this renewal clause and the amount of the rent. If the Parties cannot agree as to the amount of the Rent, the amount of the Rent will be determined by mediation.

Tenant Improvements

22. The Tenant will obtain written permission from the Landlord before doing any of the following:

   a. applying adhesive materials, or inserting nails or hooks in walls or ceilings other than two small picture hooks per wall;

   b. painting, wallpapering, redecorating or in any way significantly altering the appearance of the Property;

   c. removing or adding walls, or performing any structural alterations;

   d. installing a waterbed(s);

   e. changing the amount of heat or power normally used on the Property as well as installing additional electrical wiring or heating units;

   f. placing or exposing or allowing to be placed or exposed anywhere inside or outside the Property any placard, notice or sign for advertising or any other purpose; or

   g. affixing to or erecting upon or near the Property any radio or TV antenna or tower.

Utilities and Other Charges

23. The Landlord is responsible for the payment of the following utilities and other charges in relation to the Property: electricity, water/sewer, natural gas, garbage collection, condominium association fees and alarm/security system.

24. The Tenant is responsible for the payment of the following utilities and other charges in relation to the Property: internet.

Insurance

25. The Tenant is hereby advised and understands that the personal property of the Tenant is not insured by the Landlord for either damage or loss, and the Landlord assumes no liability for any such loss.

26. The Tenant is not responsible for insuring the Landlord's contents and furnishings in or about the Property for either damage or loss, and the Tenant assumes no liability for any such loss.

Attorney Fees

27. In the event that any action is filed in relation to this Lease, the unsuccessful Party in the action will pay to the successful Party, in addition to all the sums that either Party may be called on to pay, a reasonable sum for the successful Party's attorney fees.

Governing Law

28. This Lease will be construed in accordance with and exclusively governed by the laws of the Province of Saskatchewan.

Severability

29. If there is a conflict between any provision of this Lease and the Act, the Act will prevail and such provisions of the Lease will be amended or deleted as necessary in order to comply with the Act. Further, any provisions that are required by the Act are incorporated into this Lease.

30. The invalidity or unenforceability of any provisions of this Lease will not affect the validity or enforceability of any other provision of this Lease. Such other provisions remain in full force and effect.

Amendment of Lease

31. This Lease may only be amended or modified by a written document executed by the Parties.

Assignment and Subletting

32. The Tenant will not assign this Lease, or sublet or grant any concession or licence to use the Property or any part of the Property. Any assignment, subletting, concession, or licence, whether by operation of law or otherwise, will be void and will, at Landlord's option, terminate this Lease.

Additional Clause

33. This is a 12 month lease. Cleaning fee of $500.00 taken off Security Deposit upon Move Out for unclean unit.
Door after hours access code 1962*
Storage unit #17.

Damage to Property

34. If the Property should be damaged other than by the Tenant's negligence or willful act or that of the Tenant's employee, family, agent, or visitor and the Landlord decides not to rebuild or repair the Property, the Landlord may end this Lease by giving appropriate notice.

Care and Use of Property

35. The Tenant will promptly notify the Landlord of any damage, or of any situation that may significantly interfere with the normal use of the Property or to any furnishings supplied by the Landlord.

36. The Tenant will not engage in any illegal trade or activity on or about the Property.

37. The Parties will comply with standards of health, sanitation, fire, housing and safety as required by law.

38. The Parties will use reasonable efforts to maintain the Property in such a condition as to prevent the accumulation of moisture and the growth of mold. The Tenant will promptly notify the Landlord in writing of any moisture accumulation that occurs or of any visible evidence of mold discovered by the Tenant. The Landlord will promptly respond to any such written notices from the Tenant.

39. If the Tenant is absent from the Property and the Property is unoccupied for a period of 4 consecutive days or longer, the Tenant will arrange for regular inspection by a competent person. The Landlord will be notified in advance as to the name, address and phone number of the person doing the inspections.

40. At the expiration of the term of this Lease, the Tenant will quit and surrender the Property in as good a state and condition as they were at the commencement of this Lease, reasonable use and wear and tear excepted.

Rules and Regulations

41. The Tenant will obey all rules and regulations of the Landlord regarding the Property.

Address for Notice

42. For any matter relating to this tenancy, the Tenant may be contacted at the Property or through the phone number below:

First Tenant

    a. Name: Ashish Kumar Sharma

    b. Phone: _________________________

    c. Email: _________________________

Second Tenant

    a. Name: Shuchita Singh

    b. Phone: ███████████

    c. Email: Shuchita.08@gmail.com

43. For any matter relating to this tenancy, whether during or after this tenancy has been terminated, the Landlord's address for notice is:

    a. Name: ███████████

    b. Address: ███████████████

    The contact information for the Landlord is:

    c. Phone: ███████

    d. Email address: ███████████

General Provisions

44. All monetary amounts stated or referred to in this Lease are based in the Canadian dollar.

45. Any waiver by the Landlord of any failure by the Tenant to perform or observe the provisions of this Lease will not operate as a waiver of the Landlord's rights under this Lease in respect of any subsequent defaults, breaches or non-performance and will not defeat or affect in any way the Landlord's rights in respect of any subsequent default or breach.

46. This Lease will extend to and be binding upon and inure to the benefit of the respective heirs, executors, administrators, successors and assigns, as the case may be, of each Party. All covenants are to be construed as conditions of this Lease.

47.   All sums payable by the Tenant to the Landlord pursuant to any provision of this Lease will be deemed to be additional rent and will be recovered by the Landlord as rental arrears.

48.   Where there is more than one Tenant executing this Lease, all Tenants are jointly and severally liable for each other's acts, omissions and liabilities pursuant to this Lease.

49.   Locks may not be added or changed without the prior written agreement of both Parties, or unless the changes are made in compliance with the Act.

50.   The Tenant will be charged an additional amount of $25.00 for each N.S.F. cheque or cheques returned by the Tenant's financial institution.

51.   If the Tenant moves out prior to the natural expiration of this Lease, liquidated damages of $2,850.00 will be charged to the Tenant.

52.   Headings are inserted for the convenience of the Parties only and are not to be considered when interpreting this Lease. Words in the singular mean and include the plural and vice versa. Words in the masculine mean and include the feminine and vice versa.

53.   This Lease may be executed in counterparts. Facsimile signatures are binding and are considered to be original signatures.

54.   This Lease constitutes the entire agreement between the Parties.

55.   During the last 30 days of this Lease, the Landlord or the Landlord's agents will have the privilege of displaying the usual 'For Sale' or 'For Rent' or 'Vacancy' signs on the Property.

56.   Time is of the essence in this Lease.

IN WITNESS WHEREOF Ashish Kumar Sharma and Shuchita Singh and Louac Investments Inc. have duly affixed their signatures on this 8th day of June, 2022.

Louac Investments Inc.

Per: _______________________________ (Seal)

____
Ashish Kumar Sharma

____
Shuchita Singh

The Tenant acknowledges receiving a duplicate copy of this Lease signed by the Tenant and the Landlord on the ___8___ day of _____June_____, 20__22__

____
Ashish Kumar Sharma

____
Shuchita Singh

Be careful about setting up an auto-debit payment mechanism, as it is at the mercy of the payee and you have to pay your bank to stop it. When we moved from one rental to another, we suffered a loss of a month's rent on account of one of our lease conditions. Although our landlord was not entitled to deduct any money from our security deposit on any random pretext, he did so. When we talked to people about it, we learnt that there was a proper channel through which you could raise a complaint about the non-refunded security money: the Saskatchewan Office of Residential Tenancies (ORT), which takes care of all tenancy-related complaints. Its site mentions all the protocols tenants and owners should follow. Registering on the site takes a bit of time, but it will pay off in the long run.

We dropped a mail to the ORT and found out that landlords cannot use security money to pay for carpet cleaning or other such services. There are clear guidelines that specify the rights of tenants. Therefore, we filed a complaint with all the necessary documentation. The complaint was reviewed and then approved. A hearing date was assigned and we—the tenants—and the landlord received summons. The landlord was told to deposit the pending money with the ORT. On the day of the hearing, the judge decided the money was to be returned to us. We won the case.

Do remember to sign the move-in inspection and move-out inspection.

Sample Move out Notice

Moving Out Notice

Cleaning Your Apartment

The person whose name is on the lease is responsible for the cleaning of the apartment when moving out. Attached to this letter is a cleaning checklist to follow in order to get a full security deposit back.

Returning keys to an uncleaned apartment **will result in charges** to your security deposit for cleaning fees.

If, for whatever reason, you are unable to clean your apartment, please contact the Building Manager ███████████████████ in advance and request that the apartment be cleaned by a cleaning service. There is a charge for this service that will vary based on the size and condition of your apartment.

Move Out Walk Through Appointment

Please note that the removal of all your items and cleaning of the apartment **must be completed by 12:00 noon on the last day of the month.** No exceptions are considered.

Contact ███████████████████ one week in advance to schedule your walk through.

The walk through can take up to 30 minutes to complete and is necessary to receive your security deposit refund. Please arrange for all your items to be moved and cleaning to be complete before your walk through.

**Walk throughs cannot be arranged on the day you move out. Waiting to make an appointment on the last day of the month will result in the Building Manager unable to complete your walkout, and a delay in your security deposit refund.

Key FOB and Mail Key Return

All keys need to be returned upon the move out inspection. Any keys not returned will be charged a replacement fee.

Replacement Fee Prices:

$75.00/key – replacement mail keys
$50.00/key – replacement key FOBS

Painting and Wall Repair

If a tenant damages walls in a unit and they require repair or repaint, the following charges will be applied. The amount covers reasonable, but not excessive (ie: large holes in the wall) repairs. Excessive repairs will result in additional charges.

Whole Unit Charges

1 Bedroom Apartment	$900.00
2 Bedroom Apartment	$975.00

Individual Wall Charges

1 Wall	$150.00
2 Walls	$200.00
3 Walls	$250.00
1 Bedroom (4+ walls)	$300.00 +

Additional Charges

Hole or chip in wall up to 6 inches plus painting	$150.00/wall
Hole in wall larger than 6 inches	$175.00/hole plus painting
Mounted TV wall repair	$200.00 plus painting
Furniture Removal	$75.00 per piece

Move Out Checklist

If you cannot clean your apartment please contact your Building Manager ████████████████

Please do not throw furniture in or around the disposal bins, or charges for furniture removal will apply.

Kitchen

Cupboards/cabinets/drawers, countertops, sinks	- Clean with bleach, degreaser, or all purpose cleaner
Cabinet Doors	- Degreased and streak free on the outside - Wiped down on the inside
Fridge	- Pulled out from the wall, swept and mopped - Cleaned inside with all-purpose cleaner or bleach - Freezer defrosted and cleaned inside - Stainless steel to be cleaned and streak free
Stove	- Pull out from the wall, swept and mopped - Inside cleaned with oven cleaner (or use self-cleaning option and wipe clean) - Top cleaned and scraped clean of any burnt material - Stainless steel to be cleaned and streak free
Microwave	- Inside wiped clean with all-purpose cleaner or bleach - Went hood under the microwave is also to be wiped clean - Fan filter pulled out, washed clean, and returned - Stainless steel to be cleaned and streak free

Bathroom

Bathtub	- Cleaned with all-purpose cleaner or bleach (include tub surround) - Shower head, taps, faucet cleaned and streak free
Sink	- Cleaned and sanitized with all-purpose cleaner or bleach - Taps and faucets cleaned and streak free
Vanity and Door	- Cleaned and sanitized with all-purpose cleaner or bleach
Mirror	- Cleaned with glass cleaner and streak free
Toilet	- Cleaned and sanitized inside - Outside leaned and sanitized with all-purpose cleaner or bleach
Exhaust Vent	- Pulled down, washed out, returned

Laundry Room

Washer/Dryer	- Cleaned and sanitized with all-purpose cleaner or bleach inside and out - Lint trap cleaned out - Empty of clothes - Floor swept and mopped - Door wiped down

Bedrooms

Closets	- Clean inside walls and the doors with all all-purpose cleaner or bleach
Heat vents	- Wiped down and free of dust and stains
Windows	- Cleaned with glass cleaner and streak free - Window frames wiped down with all-purpose cleaner or bleach
Blinds	- Wiped down and free of dust

Carpets (if applicable)	- Mandatory carpet cleaning charges are (if applicable):
	
	  1 bedroom $130.00
	  2 bedroom $150.00
	  3 bedroom $160.00
	- Tenants that have their carpets cleaned professionally must provide a receipt upon move out to avoid this charge

Walls	- Cleaned and sanitized with all-purpose cleaner or bleach - Any stickers removed (or repainting charges apply)

Living/Dining Room

Balcony (if applicable)	- Clean the area - Sweep debris, pick up garbage, clean outside glass with window cleaner - Clean any traces of pet waste (failure to do so will result in charge to pressure wash the balcony) - Heat vents wiped down and free of dust or stains - Air conditioning unit cleaned and dust free
Floor	- Cleaned and sanitized with all-purpose cleaner or bleach
Baseboards	- Cleaned and sanitized with all-purpose cleaner or bleach
Walls	- Cleaned and sanitized with all-purpose cleaner or bleach - Any stickers removed (or repainting charges apply)
Doors and Light Switches	- Cleaned and sanitized with all-purpose cleaner or bleach

Estimated cleaning charges:

Balcony $25.00: Clean and sweep balcony and ensure it is free of debris.

Bathroom $85.00: Clean with diluted bleach or all purpose cleaner (ex. Mr. Clean) the bathtub, tub tiles, toilet, sink, vanity, mirror, soap dish, shower rod, all faucets, tissue holders, and clean exhaust fan/vent.

Closets $30.00: Clean storage room, linen, entrance and bedroom closets.

Cupboards $75.00: Clean and wipe with all purpose cleaner the inside and outside of cupboards, top of cupboards, countertops and sink.

Dishwasher $30.00: Clean inside and out with all purpose cleaning solution. If there is a removable filter inside, at the bottom, remove it, clean it and replace. To remove filter- twist counter clockwise.

Fixtures $30.00: Wash all light fixtures with all purpose cleaner and replace all burnt out bulbs, including exterior fixtures.

Floor Coverings $75.00: All linoleum areas must be washed with all purpose cleaner. All carpeted areas must be vacuumed. All baseboards must be cleaned with all purpose cleaner including doors, windowsills and frames. Carpets will be professionally steam cleaned and the cost of it will be deducted from the tenant's security deposit.

Fridge $60.00: Defrost, clean inside and out with diluted bleach or all purpose cleaner, pull out and clean all exterior sides and the floor underneath with all purpose cleaner, replace burnt out bulb. Leave fridge shut off with door open.

Microwave $30.00: Clean inside and out with all purpose cleaner.

Misc $60.00: Clean air-conditioner and heat radiators. Remove cover and vacuum the fins, and the carpet underneath.

Stove $75.00: Clean inside of oven with oven cleaner – unless stove is self cleaning then use that option and wipe clean. Clean with all purpose cleaner the burners, under burners, hood and fan. Replace burnt out oven bulb. Pull out and clean all exterior sides and the floor underneath.

Walls $155.00: Wash all walls with diluted bleach or all purpose cleaner.

Washer/Dryer $30.00: Clean exterior with all purpose cleaner.

Windows $60.00: Clean inside and out of windows and doors, including window tracks, replace dismounted drapery tracks.

Tip: Bedrooms in Canada have carpets—not floor rugs. The floor is itself completely carpeted, like offices in India. We don't have such carpeting in Indian houses. When you move out in Canada, you have to pay extra to clean the carpeted floors and you have to be careful not to stain them.

When we shifted to an independent house, we had to have the power and gas connections registered in our names. In Canada, you have to explicitly transfer utilities like electricity and gas to tenants' names, which is not needed if you are renting a house in India. The process for it is simple: you need to create an account online, log in and request the transfer. You will be charged a small fee for this. When you rent an independent house, you need to get insured as well. The landlord or dealer will tell you about all the requirements, so make sure you have clarity on everything before you say yes. Moving in and moving out are not child's play. They are taken very seriously.

Scotiabank®   Payroll Direct Deposit Instructions

Please complete and submit this form to your employer to have your paycheque automatically deposited into your Scotiabank account.

To: ____
(INSERT NAME OF YOUR EMPLOYER)

Please accept these instructions to automatically deposit my paycheque into my bank account as outlined below:

Employee Information

EMPLOYEE NAME
MRS SHUCHITA SINGH

CITY
AURORA

PROVINCE
ON

POSTAL CODE
L4G3M4

EMPLOYEE NUMBER (IF APPLICABLE)   DEPARTMENT (IF APPLICABLE)

Employee Bank Account Information

INSTITUTION
THE BANK OF NOVA SCOTIA

NUMBER   12 DIGIT ACCOUNT NUMBER

Company Processing Instructions ▶   Enter as TRANSIT No.   Enter as ACCOUNT No.

BRANCH ADDRESS

I am advising the Company to change my payroll direct deposit as indicated above. I understand that Scotiabank is not responsible for verifying these payments to my account. I will notify the Company promptly in writing if I close or make other changes to my account.

Authorized by:

___________________________   2023-JUL-06
SIGNATURE   DATE

Please forward the completed request to the appropriate department in your company. Some employers may also ask you to attach a voided cheque. You may wish to keep a copy of the completed form for your records.

1662613 (02/10)   ® Registered trademark of The Bank of Nova Scotia

Driving Licence

The world is divided into countries with left-hand drive and countries with right-hand drive. India is a left-hand-drive country, whereas western countries like the US and Canada are right-hand-drive countries, which means the driver sits on the left side in the car. For those of us from left-hand-drive countries, getting a driving licence in Canada can be a challenge, as you have to reorient things in your mind. When you have been driving for more than eight to ten years in India, it becomes really difficult to unlearn your habits and then learn new ones.

Unlearning is the bigger problem. I had been driving for years in India, so you could call me an expert driver by Indian standards, and the same was the case with Ashish, but, as he had developed the dizziness issue, I had to clear the driving test and get a driving licence as soon as possible. It would be winter soon and we would need to move around in a car, especially with the kids.

Getting the driving licence felt like nothing less than climbing Mount Everest. Firstly, the process was not very clear, due to which we lost a significant amount of time. There are two stages: a written test and then a road test. The written test, which must be prepared for using a PDF available online, can be taken on any day except for Sunday. No appointments need to be made. You just need to pay the fee at a counter and get your eyes checked. **Tip: if you wear glasses, carry them with you and declare that you wear them, as you cannot drive without glasses. Your driving licence will state that you wear glasses as a condition.** As soon as the formalities are completed, you will be assigned a system in which you will have to take the online test. All the questions are straightforward MCQs from the study material and, as soon as you finish, you get your result. You must score more than 80% to pass. If you pass, then you get your learner's licence immediately. But if you fail, then you can either prepare more or re-attempt it right away. You can attempt the test as many times as you want in a day if you are willing to keep paying.

But before doing all this, you need to create an identification card, for which you need to create a login ID on the Saskatchewan Government

Insurance (SGI) website and then contact a motor issuer agency (we contacted Affinity Insurance) to book an appointment for the creation of the ID. On the day of the appointment, they take documents like copies of your passport, lease agreement, etc., take a photo of you when you reach their office and issue a temporary ID until the card gets delivered to you by mail.[20] Once you have the ID, you can apply for your driving licence (this is not the case in Ontario, where you can directly apply for a licence).

We made a mistake here. Firstly, we didn't know an ID had to be created. We thought we could apply directly for the licence. Later, when we learnt about the necessity of an ID, we ran into a lot of confusion over the required documents. Some said possessing a health card was mandatory, whereas some said this was not the case. We were waiting for our health cards at the time. This confusion added to the time our application process took. After making multiple calls, we went to a motor issuer, who was fine with the COPR, passport and lease agreement.

Motor issuer agencies provide a range of services—your ID, number plate, car registration, car insurance and home insurance, to name a few. The number plate is linked to your car insurance and your car registration. As soon as you register a vehicle, a default insurance plan kicks in, which is mandatory. You can increase the insurance coverage over and above this default plan. There is no concept of a temporary number; you get your permanent number plate as soon as you register your vehicle. You can choose the type of number plate and can even customise it with a six-character string of your choice. This was quite amazing to me—you can print your name or the name of your child or anyone you love on your number plate!

---

20 Please note that this refers to postal mail and not e-mail.

We cleared the written test on our first attempts. Most people take at least four or five attempts to pass it. That boosted our confidence. The next barrier was the road test, for which you have to book an appointment. Your slot may be a month away, so don't wait to be a perfect driver before you book your test. **Book the test first, then keep practising.**

I passed my road test after failing five times. After the failures, I realised my trainer was no good. He had actually not told me about aspects of driving in Canada that were important. Ashish, who risked taking the test between my failed attempts while he was still feeling dizzy and passed on his first attempt, taught me instead and I also took the help of professional drivers' videos. So don't go with cheap trainers. Hire certified ones. We had to pay huge amounts unnecessarily as test booking fees and road test charges to hire a car.

I felt later that it was a good thing I had failed. My basics were very weak. I would have taken to the roads with those weak basics and surely got in big trouble. My failures helped me strengthen my basics. I finally started driving solo on March 21, 2023.

NOTE: There is a way to obtain at least the Ontario G2 Driving Licence immediately, if not the G1. However, for this, you need to do certain things before you fly. You can look up the details online.

All about driving licence, car, insurance, etc. → https://www. mysgi.ca/

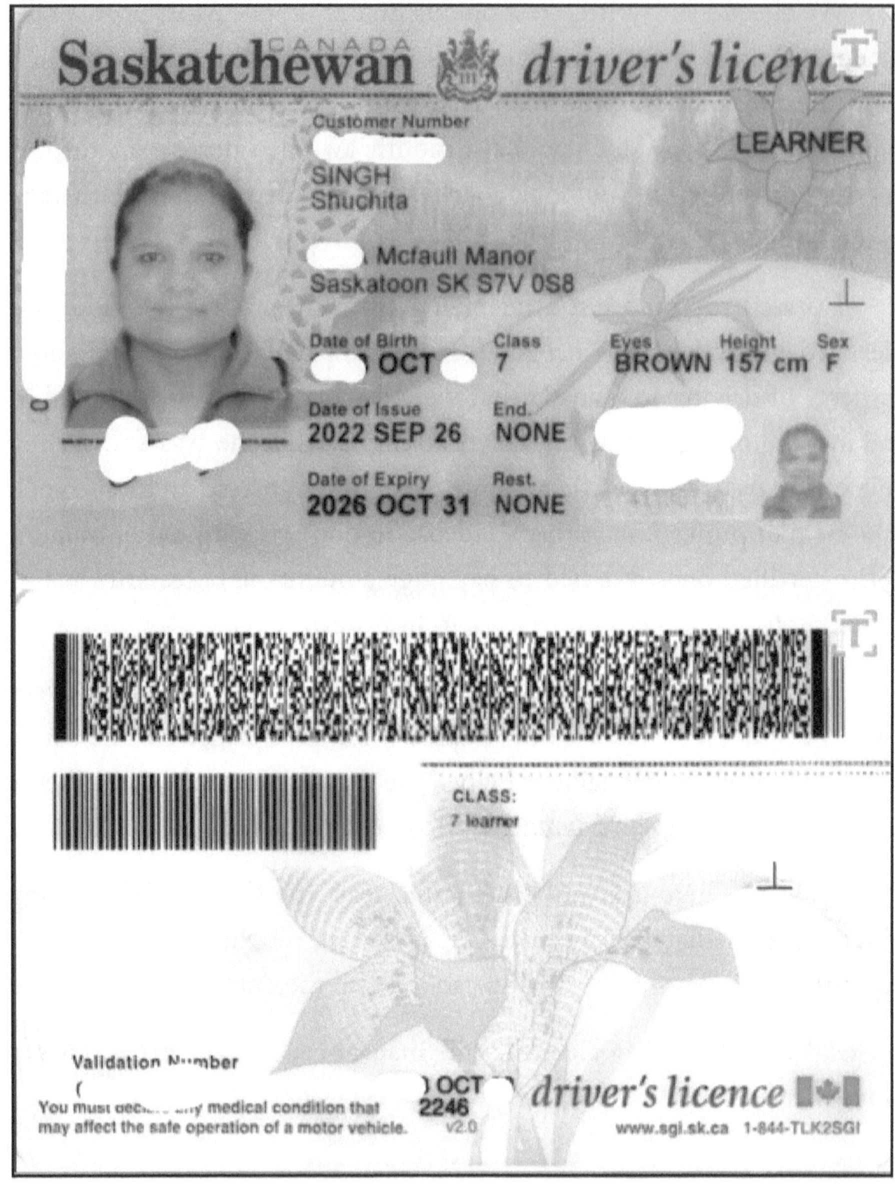

Car on Lease

In India, people who have cars own them. Leasing has never been an option. The term 'lease' was only heard in this context when a vehicle was provided by one's company. However, in Canada, leasing a car is very common. People lease cars for four years or more, paying a biweekly EMI. **All payments are biweekly in Canada: EMIs, salaries, gym memberships, furniture rentals, everything.**

When you go to a showroom in India, you are served water, tea, coffee and what not, but in Canada, be prepared to not be served anything. This is the case not only with automobile showrooms but also with property visits. Get used to it. We were so used to being offered *kachori* and *samosa* that we took it for granted when we were in India. Now I understand the meaning of *mehmannavaji*.[21] My respect for Indian culture and customs has grown since I have been exposed to the other side of the world. It's almost mandatory in India to serve water and then tea/coffee if someone visits your home. Even shops and showrooms have the same culture. Here, I experienced a cultural shift. Nobody even asks whether you want water!

All the formalities for registering a car can be completed on the SGI website. There are various services you can opt for, including snow tyres. Canada's winter is so harsh that you need special tyres to deal with the snow. Thus, there are two types of tyres—all-season and winter tyres. The cars here are actually as smart as Transformers. I am not exaggerating—cars alert you if you are touching the edges of your lane and re-adjust themselves, display the speed limit of the road you are on, have sophisticated controls for seat adjustment and heating systems that allow you to heat your seat and steering wheel and can be started remotely with the help of an app. It is very common in Canada to start and warm up the car before you actually hop in. Windshield covers are used to save time by those who only have access to stilt parking— without a cover, in order to drive your car you will need 15–20 extra minutes to clean the snow off it and defrost the windshield for visibility. Snow corrodes cars more rapidly than other weather conditions, so

---

21 Hospitality

there are various techniques to help fight this, including Corrosion Control Module, undercoating, ceramic paint protection, clear paint film protection, etc.

SGI provides you with a basic insurance plan as soon as you register, but every car has its own minimum insurance requirements that you have to fulfil. Roadside assistance is also provided, as in India. The coverage offered is substantial. If your car breaks down and it will take more than 24 hours to fix, you will be provided with a vehicle for that time period.

Remember that you must have a driving licence to purchase a vehicle. So clear the road test or at least get a learner's licence (by clearing the written test) before buying a car.

Identity Card

This is a non-photo ID that you need to make before even applying for a driving licence. Actually, this is the first of the identity proofs that you will need, although that may vary based on province.

You can have it made for you at any motor licence issuer's office. Search for the nearest one, walk in with your passport, COPR and health card and the formalities will be taken care of. It hardly takes any time and the hard copy of the card gets delivered to you by mail.

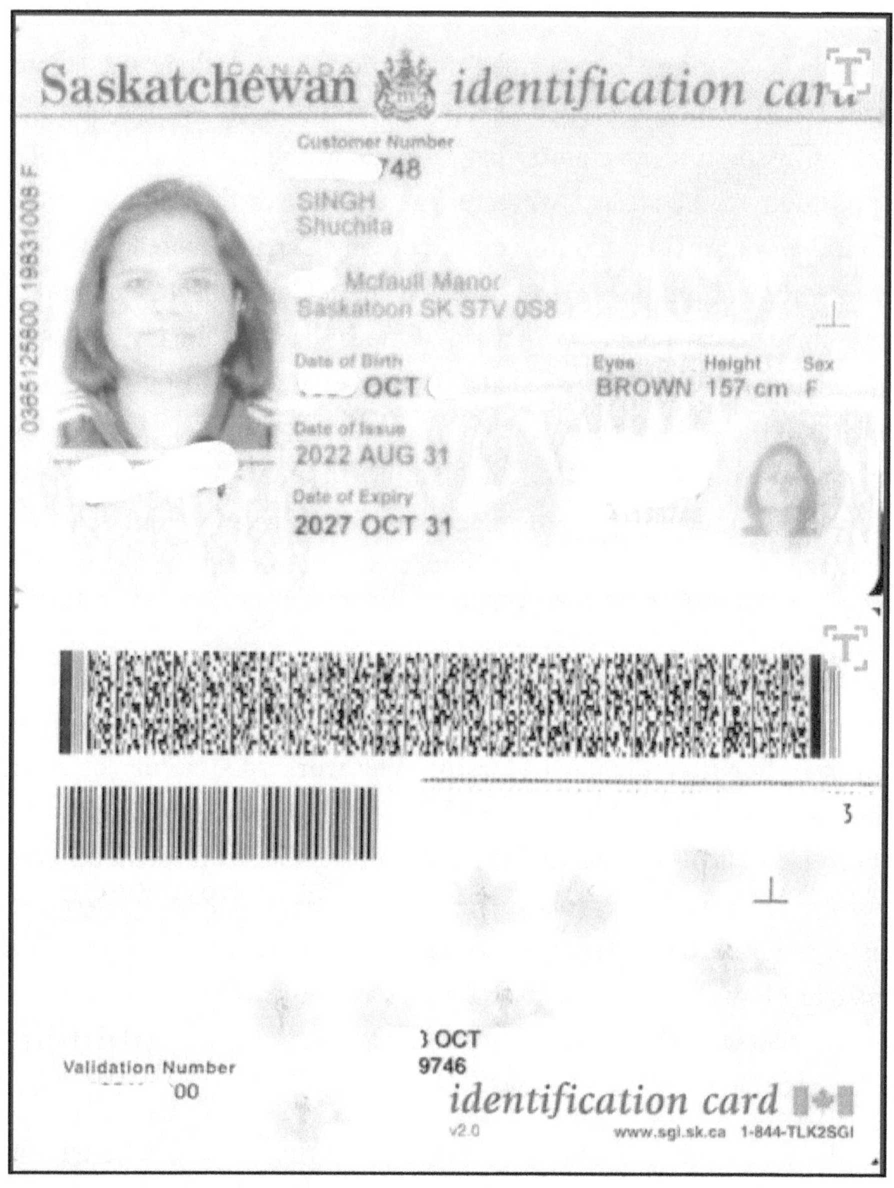

Get your identity card → https://sgi.sk.ca/photo-id

Jobs

Canada is a country with a small population. Hence, there is a labour crunch here, which is why Canada promotes immigration. Immigration helps Canada run the country better, while immigrants cash in on the opportunity to be abroad, whatever the reasons for their immigration. So it does not matter why you moved or why Canada invited you to be there—the bottom line is that, once you are in Canada, you must have a job. There are two possible scenarios. One is that you already secured a job while you were in India. That's the best-case scenario, but only 10% of the people who come to Canada are fortunate in this regard. On the other hand, if you need to find a job after landing in Canada, which is the case with most people, there are again two ways of doing so. Either you wait to get a job related to your stream or you do secondary jobs until you get the job of your choice.

People usually work secondary jobs—jobs that are not of their own stream or skill set. These are odd jobs that people take up for survival. For example, an IT person may work as a cashier or store manager or at a gas station or a McDonald's or Starbucks. This way, they won't eat into their savings and will be able to feed themselves until they land a better job. In Canada, no job is looked down on, so there is no social pressure to not take up a certain type of job. The only hindrance is mental. If you are able to overcome that, you can easily meet your daily needs until you bag your first job in the stream of your choice.

To find a job in Canada is itself a skill. You need to take on any job you get to build work experience in Canada and slowly make your way forward. People from IT or software backgrounds are the ones who get a job with comparative ease, whereas people with other skill sets, like mechanical or electrical expertise, have a tougher time, especially if they previously occupied senior-level posts in India. People with less experience can easily figure their way out after getting several licences, as Canada requires individuals to possess certain licences in order to work professionally in streams like electrical engineering, finance, etc. Be ready to learn. Open yourself up to the challenge and say, 'Yes, I can do it.'

Your job is the sphere in which you will have to make the biggest compromises initially. Only slowly and steadily will you be able to get back to the level you were at when you left India. **The job struggle period will be longer than your settlement period.** I believe it takes a minimum of a year to settle personally and two years to settle professionally. The key is to keep changing your resume according to the job posting. Make sure your resume is in the approved Canadian format and try getting referrals by building Canadian connections.

I have also heard, but am not sure, that career development is a bit slower in Canada than it is in India. India has better prospects in terms of raises, designations and opportunities. But Canada is a country where handy-workers are really scarce, so if you are an electrician or plumber or a junior engineer, you will be able to sort things out for yourself faster than experienced professionals, who will have to compromise on their designation and type of work.

Meanwhile, the key to personal settlement is to mingle with everyone. Don't confine yourself to your own community. Your own community gives you that homely feeling, but expanding your contacts gives you the chance to see the world through others' eyes. You learn what to say and how to say it and you come to know a variety of people, which impacts your life in one way or another.

Buying a House

It is commonly believed that buying a house is easier than renting one, as EMIs are less than rent amounts. That was the case maybe five or ten years ago, but, with increased interest rates, it isn't so anymore. Buy a home only when your pocket allows it. Even before you start looking for a new house, you need to have yourself evaluated as a buyer. For this, you need to approach a mortgage broker, who will ask for various details, like your bank balance, a bank certificate for money in India, credit reports, etc. On the basis of these documents, the broker will let you know what your upper limit is, what kind of loan you are eligible for and how much you will need to pay as a down payment. If you haven't built up your credit score yet, then you may have to pay 10% as down payment; if you have, it could be 5%. This depends on various circumstances.

Once you get a budget, you can start working with a realtor. Canada has different houses even within the same neighbourhoods, unlike India, where societies tend to have similar houses in terms of structure or exteriors. On the other hand, you could say that independent houses (which are not part of a society) in India are the same as they are in Canada in terms of exteriors, i.e. different from each other.

The basic types of houses are as follows:

1. Detached: a house that does not share its walls with any other house.
2. Townhouse: independent, but with a shared wall.
3. Condos: flats in a multi-storey building. Everything within one flat is on the same floor.

Usually, what is different about detached homes in Canada compared to those in India in terms of interiors is that the ones in Canada follow a common pattern: basement, ground floor, first floor, laundry, mechanical room, etc.

Sample Floor Plans –

Main Floor

Second Floor

Optional Basement Development

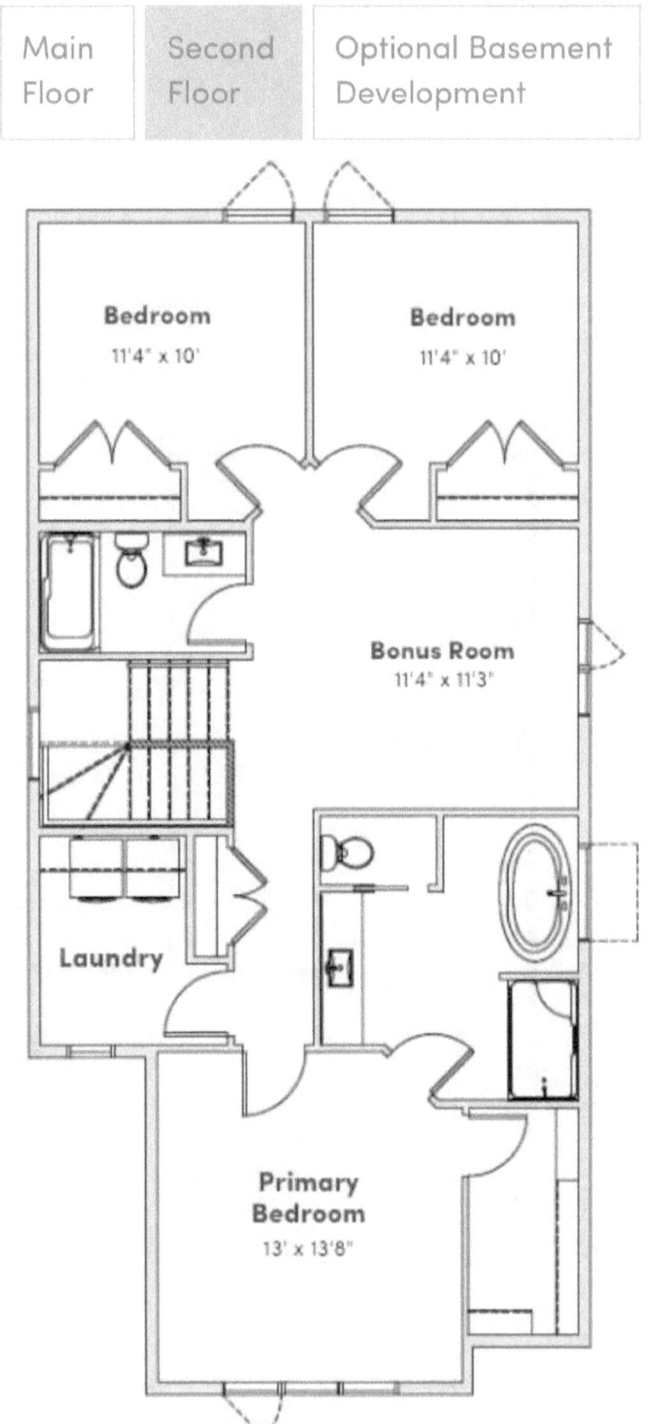
Main Floor
Second Floor
Optional Basement Development
Bedroom
11'4" x 10'
Bedroom
11'4" x 10'
Bonus Room
11'4" x 11'3"
Laundry
Primary Bedroom
13' x 13'8"

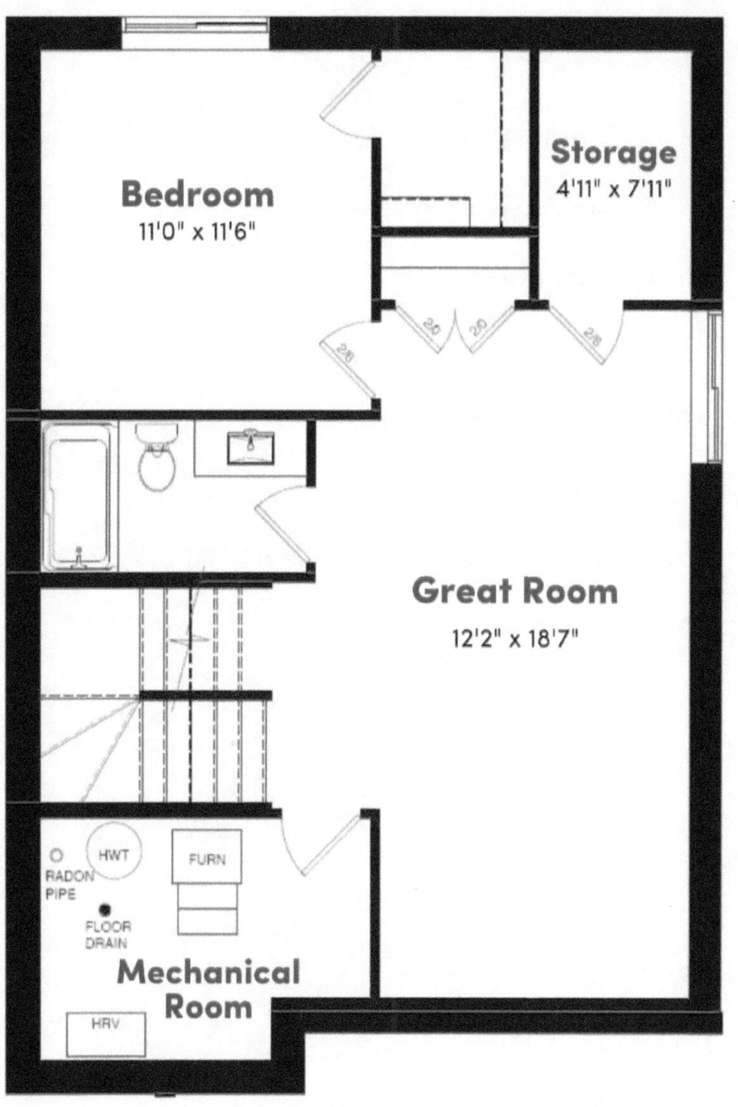
Main Floor
Second Floor
Optional Basement Development
Bedroom
11'0" x 11'6"
Storage
4'11" x 7'11"
Great Room
12'2" x 18'7"
HWT
RADON PIPE
FURN
FLOOR DRAIN
Mechanical Room
HRV

Experiencing Canada

Experiencing Canada means living in Canada. How do you feel when…

… you perform your daily chores?

… you shop or do your groceries?

… when you visit the salon?

… when you go to a mall?

… when you are at work?

… when you are at home?

… when your child comes home from school?

… when you get sick?

… when you drive or walk around?

Do you feel…

… secure?

… cared for?

… respected?

… free?

… touched by the warmth of others?

… free from chaos?

… worried?

… under pressure?

… that balancing work life and personal life is a struggle?

What is your career outlook? Are you happy being in Canada? Or do you feel disconnected, disheartened, undervalued, uprooted?

The answers to the above questions will decide whether you continue living in Canada or move back, so it's very important to evaluate how you feel about being in Canada. Below, I have described my experience of Saskatoon. Please note that each city might produce different experiences.

Salon

When we moved, we heard that the service sector was pricey in Canada, so we initially avoided salons. However, the change in climate caused me to experience severe hair fall, like that of a cancer patient. We were told that extreme cold leads to dandruff and then hair fall. Although we reached Canada in May, which is officially summer, being new to the climate, we found it to be like winter in India.

Anyway, one fine day I decided to get a haircut, so I visited a salon downstairs and enquired about their rates and how it works. I learnt that you cannot just walk in whenever you wish. You need to make an appointment to get your hair done. That was annoying. I had never ever made an appointment for a haircut. Towards the end of our time in India, we had to start checking for the availability of our favourite hairstylist but it was possible to get an appointment on the same day with just a text or a call. It was never very formal.

But, in Canada, there is a process for getting an appointment with a hairstylist. You need to go to the salon's website and pick a professional with whom you would like to fix your appointment. Professionals or salon artists are priced based on their skills and experience, which are detailed on the website. The price of a service increases with the experience of the professional, so while there are base rates, the final cost is calculated based on the stylist you opt for.

There are also various aspects to the cost that are mentioned explicitly, like consultation, which in India is kind of complementary. And yes, these services are pricey. I booked a haircut with a not-so-experienced stylist, and I was charged around $70 (Rs 4,200).

After you pick the service and the stylist, you need to choose the date and time. If the stylist is in demand, then you may get an appointment for a month later. If the salon is not too popular, then you may get an appointment the next day. Getting an appointment on the same day, however, is entirely a matter of luck.

Salons follow office hours, which means you cannot get a haircut after your office timings. Rather, you need to fit your appointment into your work hours. I found this very strange. In India, you go for haircuts in your leisure time, usually late in the evening after work. But, in Canada, it's more formal, and this is the case with other activities as well. It's not like you won't get anything in the late evening, but for stores to remain open is not very common. In India, malls and shops stay open by default until nine or ten p.m. every day, and we would go to any shop irrespective of the time. In Canada, however, you cannot go to many of the shops and malls in the evening. **Check the timings of the mall on Google before you decide whether to go or not.**

Anyway, returning to the salon, the stylist heard about my hair fall problem and said, 'Your hair looks perfectly healthy, but it seems to have been affected by the weather. So take natural care of it. Nothing additional is required.' I kept asking her if she had suggestions for shampoos, conditioners or hair services that would help, but all she said was, 'No.'

That was another shocking part of my salon visit. If I had been in India, I would have been recommended the most expensive shampoo and conditioner on the shelf. The shampoo I was using would have been blamed for my dandruff and hair fall. I would have surely been recommended a hair spa treatment for more strength. I would have been treated as a person who needed a lot of attention to look beautiful, someone who had neglected herself. In contrast, the stylist in the salon under our apartment in Canada said, 'You have beautiful hair.'

It had always annoyed me about Indian salons that the stylists made you feel less valued and less beautiful, constantly suggesting that you needed one thing or another. I always needed to prepare myself to say 'No' to endless recommendations of services by the salon artist.

But there was a twist. As soon as she started with my hair, she began asking me about every single thing. 'How short' is an obvious question, but she asked me about each step, which gave me the impression that either she didn't know much or she was seeking my approval, which was a bit annoying. In India, we leave the haircut to the stylist after briefly telling them what we want.

I have had multiple haircuts now and I must say they feel better in Canada. You are told that you are beautiful even if you don't avail of any of the salon's services. Whether you do or not is your wish. It is not something you are pressured into. You will get great service, but it will be expensive for sure.

Canada has a culture of tipping, but I was so awed by the $70 charge that I didn't offer a tip. It's common for people to ask for tips everywhere, even when you take a cab and pay the fair. But don't hesitate to say no if you don't want to pay the tip. That's perfectly alright.

I am yet to try other services, but I have noticed that not all salons do everything. Some offer only hair services, some only do nails (nail art is very common in Canada), some do brow work and some may offer everything.

A service that intrigued me was 'brow tinting', which involves colouring eyebrows and giving them shape. I was shocked when I saw people who had had it done. I couldn't figure out what was wrong with them at first but was amazed to later find out what it was.

Malls

As soon as we think of malls, parking struggles come to mind—the chaos we go through trying to find a spot. Parking in India is a saga in itself, a time-consuming affair that can consume up to two hours— finding a spot to park, getting from the parking space to the mall itself, and then waiting to get out of parking… Moreover, you have to pay for it, often on an hourly basis. Parking can be the factor that determines whether you visit a particular place or not.

The experience at Canadian malls is the opposite. There is no paid parking. Parking is free and it is a piece of cake. You just shoot in and out in the blink of an eye. Parking is no more a factor in decisions about going anywhere. It's very rare that you even need to search for a spot. That only happens on sale days or days like Black Friday.

Anyway, we have spent enough time on 'parking'. Let's go inside the mall now.

Though shopping or window-shopping has always been relaxing, doing it in Canada seems like therapy. Malls are sooo quiet and crowd-free that you initially feel like the mall has opened just for you (although not in the big cities of Ontario). In India, malls are not as sparsely populated even during office hours.

Of course, the kinds of items that are available in the mall are different from what is available in India, but what I noticed was the difference in the quality of things. Everything seems to be high quality, whereas even Chinese products do not look like Chinese products when they are sold in India.

If you are vegetarian, you will struggle a bit in the food courts. However, even people here are turning vegetarian now, so you have options—just not as many as in Indian malls.

The MRP is usually not mentioned on products. Rather, shelves are labelled with the prices of the items on them. This sometimes makes it difficult to tell what the price of a particular item is.

Malls here also have sale periods, and the discounts are quite handsome, so you can plan your shopping accordingly. Here you can actually shop during sales, whereas in India it's nearly impossible to do so because it gets too crowded and you have to first struggle to pick items and then wait in long queues to make the payment. But here, sale days are like any normal day in an Indian mall during office hours.

The best part of the shopping experience in Canada is that most stores have very good return policies, offering you money back through your method of payment. If you purchase something using a credit card, then you just have to tap the card while returning the item and the money will be refunded. COSTCO offers a 90-day return window with no questions asked. What's most surprising is that food items can be returned, even if they've been opened or used a bit, in case you don't like the taste or anything like that.

I was amazed by this policy and the faith in customers that it reflects. Even at The Body Shop, you can purchase and then use a shampoo and return it within a month if you don't like it!

And if that isn't enough, there's more. Shops are lane-free... you don't need to stand in lines to make your purchase! Salespeople don't cling to you or pursue you to convince you to purchase anything. They just assist you and help you find what you need.

Frozen Foods

Canada seems to be a land of frozen foods. Earlier, I could not understand why big freezers were needed at home. I had only heard of them and seen them in Hollywood movies. Now, in Canada, I understand the need for big freezers. Canada grows very few types of food on its own. Most of its fruits, vegetables and other food items are imported from other countries. Due to this, there are lots of frozen options, including pizzas.

Yes, we always considered pizza junk food, but now we're talking about frozen pizza. You probably think it's unacceptable. I too had the same thought when I first saw it. Then I thought of trying it, or at least keeping it as backup for when I didn't feel like cooking. When I tried my first frozen pizza, I was amazed at how good it turned out to be. I am not kidding, it was really good. As good as fresh pizza. What a surprise! Now I accept frozen pizza.

Next, I came across frozen chillies. Yes, green chillies. I had never heard of frozen green chillies. Maybe we belong to a country where everything is fresh and readily available all through the year and that's why we have never thought of experimenting with frozen options. I have always wanted peas in every season, so frozen peas came to my rescue in Canada and they were as fresh and good as they could possibly be. Similarly, I have seen a wide range of frozen foods:

1. Cauliflower
2. Beans
3. Mixed vegetables
4. All types of fruits
5. All types of starters
6. *Naan, parantha,*[22] stuffed *naan*

---

22 *Parantha* is a type of Indian flatbread.

Usually, these items come in packaging that is bigger and more user-friendly than in India, such that the food can be used, then kept back in the freezer and re-used in the same packaging.

As Canada is a multicultural country, a wide range of flavours is available, including all the Indian spices, Chinese and European items, etc. You will surely find something related to any cuisine you can name in the stores here. So the grocery store is a fun zone, at least for two years, after which you become used to whatever is available.

Walmart and Costco[23] will become your Big Bazaar and stores like Save-on-Foods will become your high-end grocery stores. New lines of stores that are talked about, like Canadian Tire, HomeSense, etc., are similar to Lifestyle, Home Centre, etc., in India. The only differences I have observed have to do with the weather and the way of life. As the weather in Canada is quite harsh, all clothing lines are focused on temperature-resistant clothing. Even shoe companies have a similar focus.

Thus, you see less 'normal' clothing. Instead, Canada is dominated by sportswear. Canadians love hiking, biking and all sorts of outdoor activities. You will also see many snow-related products like snowshoes, snowboards, sledges, etc. Snow was never an integral part of our Indian lifestyle, so everything related to snow seemed new to us. India is full of colours and festivals, so Indian brands are more ethnic and less weather-influenced. Sportswear has a smaller market and is usually equated with gym wear.

Home Depot is a place for all kinds of machinery and pretty much anything you can imagine in the realm of home improvement—electrical

---

23 Please note that you need to have a Mastercard to shop from Costco, as that's the only accepted mode of payment. You cannot use a Visa card, so you can either get two credit cards or stick to a Mastercard.

goods like wires, bulbs, sockets, smart lights, and appliances, plumbing and gardening tools, bathroom tiles, construction materials, curtain rods, fasteners, cabinets, drawers, ceiling fans, paints, etc. It makes sense for such a store to exist in Canada and also for it to be missing from India, as India has entire markets and a vast labour force available to address these needs. So Home Depot is like a large Indian market inside a single store. It also provides tools like carpet cleaning machines on rent and all sorts of maintenance, upgrading, cleaning, plumbing and flooring services. It's your one stop for everything you need for home maintenance or upgradation.

There are specialised stores like Cabela and Atmosphere that deal in niche products like outdoor electrical equipment and clothes for hunting, fishing, boating, camping, etc. There are even stores that deal in clothing for snowmobiles.

Meanwhile, big toy stores like Toys R Us will change your mindset from 'just toys' to 'OMG, toys!'

Schools

Adjusting to the education system in Canada involves a huge paradigm shift. India has many tiers of schools, with huge differences in the fee structures and the kinds of facilities that the schools provide. The school that your child goes to is a matter of pride; your status is directly linked with your child's school. But in Canada, almost all the schools are similar and have the same facilities, as **education until Grade 12 is free.** Schools have nothing to do with status. They are seen as a basic need and education is provided equally, with no regard for your income. There are some private or 'Catholic' schools that charge fees, but they are exceptions. There are some 'ethnic' schools as well, but not for regular education. Most kids go to the public schools, where the education is free.

NOTE: Do not assume that the Catholic schools are better than the public schools. Both are competitive in terms of education and care. In fact, some of the public schools are excellent.

You get admission to a school based on the neighbourhood you are living in, not by choice. Usually, your kids will be accepted immediately into the neighbourhood school, whether you arrive mid-term or before a new session. There may be an 'entry test', but that is to assess whether the school needs to provide the kid extra care. Even if your kids are not very good at either of the two Canadian official languages—English and/or French—by law, schools are required to admit them. Schools also assist children with basic English and communication skills. Dedicated teachers are specially assigned to provide students with basic language assistance.

Schools usually have similar infrastructure—big campuses with various facilities like water fountains, play areas, basketball courts, football fields, etc. Each neighbourhood has its own school, so students don't have to travel very far. Usually, schools are within walking distance of homes. **If not, transportation to and from school is free and safe— you do not need to worry about dropping or picking up your child from the bus stand.**

Every province (and some cities) has its own school board. All information related to the schools in each province can be viewed on the District School Board (DSB) websites. An example is the Toronto DSB: **http://www.tdsb.on.ca/**. Some provinces of Canada do have ranking systems, whereby the government ranks schools based on performance. To enrol your child in a higher-ranked school, you need to get to the neighbourhood of that school. Rent or sales costs are directly impacted by schools in this manner. For a ranking-based overview of Canadian schools, use this link: **http://www.fraserinstitute.org/reportcards/ schoolperformance/**

The Canadian education system is relaxed in comparison to that of India. It gives children the freedom to follow their own interests instead of restricting them to being a doctor or engineer. Schools do not prescribe any uniforms and do not burden children with endless homework assignments or tests. No textbook or notebook is brought back home—everything remains in school. Children have lockers to store their stuff in. **Schoolbags in Canada contain a water bottle and a lunch pack, nothing else.** A certain number of laptops is assigned to each classroom, and they need to be booked to be used by kids. Colour pencils, crayons, paint, markers, and folders are more commonly used here than in the Indian education system. It emphasises practical and experiential learning.

Sport is an integral part of the curriculum. Children are encouraged to try out all the winter sports—ice skating, skiing, ice hockey, tubing, etc. A child can easily become a professional player if so inclined. During breaks, it is mandatory for kids to go outdoors. Only in extreme conditions is an indoor recess allowed. In this way, schools help children develop a relationship with nature.

Schools do pick students with exceptional calibre to take on more advanced studies. In Saskatoon, such students are moved to SAGE (Saskatoon Public Schools Academically Gifted Education) or a programme for gifted children to accelerate their learning. However, children in Canada are groomed for life, not for the rat race. They are made independent and adventurous and are raised to be close to nature and aware of the environment. Nothing is considered too big or too small—rather, what you pursue depends on your interests and skills. The focus is on learning, so everything seems to float along smoothly without unnecessary worries about unlimited tests every week or month. This is a boon not only for kids but for parents as well. It makes parents' lives simpler and allows them to be happy. Yes, happy. Having to run after your kids all the time, getting them to complete their homework or prepare for tests—that's enough to make you unhappy. You are always worried about your child—whether they are safe in the bus, or on the way home from the bus stop, or even in school. That worry is always present at the back of your mind in India, whether you want it or not. Canadian schools relieve you of this pressure, which you realise you were living with only after it is taken away.

The teachers pay close attention to the students' behaviour. Every single issue is analysed in depth. These issues could be as small as someone pushing someone else or complaining about someone's behaviour. It can even seem a bit dramatic at first. In Indian schools, these issues are not taken so seriously or worked on. Schools, kids and teachers don't get any time to think or talk about such things.

Personal Life

What is 'personal life'? Personal life is...

> ... how you spend your day,

> ... how you send your kids to school and how you reach office,

> ... how you work,

> ... what you do when you come back from office,

> ... how you spend your leisure time,

> ... how you spend your weekend,

> ... what your idea of fun is,

> ... how you shop,

> ... what you eat,

> ... how you eat,

> ... what you wear,

> ... how much pressure you feel on a daily basis.

School and shopping have been covered in previous sections. Not let me take you through the other regular experiences of a Canadian life.

Reaching Office

No honking, no endless waits at red lights, no factoring in rush hours or peak hours, and there you are—at your office. Now, imagine your manager is *not* tracking whether you are working or taking a break. Imagine that nobody questions why you need to pick up your child during the workday. Imagine not being overloaded or pinged after hours even once and having the freedom to say yes or no to work based on your workload. Imagine having the freedom to enjoy your vacations and leaves.

Does this sound good to you?

Returning from Office

You follow strict in and out timings. You are not obliged to extend your working hours for any actual work or to give the impression of working. You are back home at the right time and you have the time to make dinner, sit with your family, enjoy a movie or pursue your hobbies.

Leisure Time

You aren't caught up in an endless search for parking at malls. Going to malls and restaurants or going out of station are not considered leisure time activities. **Rather, leisure time is family time.** Leisure time is a walk to the park to see your kids playing. Leisure is nature—a visit to a lake or a hike or a camping trip, watching the sunrise, sunset and snowfall. Leisure is lying on your couch without worrying about time passing by. Leisure is watching the endless blue sky, following an airplane flying through it, gazing at the moon's craters. This is leisure in Canada.

Weekends

The fresh air never allows you to get tired, so you actually don't need to sleep and rest over the weekend. Rather, you use the weekend to chill. Plan a sleighing trip or a visit to a fair or a museum or anything you really want to do. You may just want to relax and do your groceries.

Weekends are usually spent socialising—having dinner or lunch together. There are always reasons to gather and celebrate—a simple drinks party, a sleepover party or maybe you haven't visited a friend of yours in a long time.

What and How to Eat

You can eat all kinds of high-quality foods and vegetables. They are actually packed pre-sorted and washed, so you can eat them with no hassles. Not having to rush while eating makes meals much more enjoyable. The food tastes the way it did when we were children, and you relive those memories while eating the best food, cooked with love, and breathe the freshest air in your beautiful, clutter-free world.

What to Wear

Clothes are not a big deal here in Canada, whereas in India, life revolves around clothes. India is blessed with such beautiful, varied weather that we can wear anything we want, but Indian clothes require you to coordinate different parts of your attire and the weather in Canada does not allow you to wear those clothes too much. Of course, you can if you want to. You wear what is comfortable to you. Nobody cares who is wearing what. You are not stared at if you wear something that is a bit revealing or showcases the shape of your body, so there is no pressure or fear to deal with while getting dressed. There is no pressure to wear new clothes or better clothes than others. I stick to what I find comfortable—any top with my favourite pants and usually a winter jacket.

Pressure

The pressure you feel on a day-to-day basis is a cumulative result of all the above factors. Now I leave it to you. Do you think you will feel stressed out, free, happy or sad in Canada?

Social Life

You will feel you are back in your childhood, when people used to visit each other, have meals together and actually chill out. Today, in India, life is so fast-paced that we have actually lost that personal touch, especially in metros. Daily chores do not allow us the luxury to pay visits to each other.

But people depend on each other for emotional and professional kinds of support, and in Canada this seems to be recognised more openly. People here usually maintain an active social circle, which gives you the freedom to chill together, travel together or have 'me time' when the kids are having their own fun. Relationships are not status-based but behaviour-based.

Living in a multicultural community broadens your perspective. You get the opportunity to meet various kinds of people from different backgrounds. I met a group of ladies who were born in India but had lived in Africa and the UK and then moved to Canada. At first, their accents sounded weird to me, as they looked no different from any other Indian. They were wearing *salwar* suits, a common Indian choice of attire, but their accents were foreign. I met them at the 'Udyapan for Laximiji Vat' in Canada, which itself sounded weird. But I was surprised at their Indianness, which, frankly speaking, might be less pronounced in people who are actually living in India. They wore lockets dedicated to Ganeshji and were very interested in singing *bhajans*[24] and doing

---

24 Religious/spiritual hymns.

achmaans[25] before meals. I could not recall having ever felt as attached to my roots. I think being abroad makes you more Indian. You start to value your culture, traditions and Indianness more.

We got invited to several lunches and dinners by our neighbours and friends and observed that people did not follow Indian stretchable time but were strict about timings.

We have a beautiful Gujarati neighbour and I saw at their place that people pack food for each other after a get-together. This is a common gesture!

Healthcare

I have already described my first medical experience in Canada and the basics of the healthcare system here, but I have realised after careful observation that doctors here don't prescribe medicines on the basis of notions. They perform thorough tests to confirm their hunch and treat the problem accordingly. They wait for a proper diagnosis to be arrived at before suggesting anything. They also tend to believe in natural healing, so they don't suggest too many supplements.

There are pros and cons to everything. You do have to wait for an appointment to see a doctor at a walk-in clinic, and this is something that someone from India will find challenging. But in India, you can be conned into an unnecessary operation or be given incorrect treatment, whereas here it's a bit more secure. On the other hand, dealing with an emergency is a challenge. You might end up waiting a whole day if you visit an ER. I have heard horror stories about people waiting endlessly and in pain. I have already recounted the story of the person who got his hand burnt and had to wait for four hours to get any sort of treatment. Another person had a nail punched into his hand, but even he had to wait.

---

25 Purification ritual involving water.

People say in real emergency situations, you should call 911 instead of walking to the ER yourself. That way, you will be provided better services. Of course, you have to pay for the ambulance, but they give you proper attention and take care of your kids as well in your absence. Also, the ambulances are highly equipped from the point of view of first aid and will reach you within a matter of minutes. So calling 911 is the fastest and most effective way of dealing with any emergency. As mentioned earlier, you will even be airlifted in a helicopter in case it is needed.

It's hard to say whether the system is bad or good. Medical facilities are government-funded, so nobody has to pay for any consultation or tests or ultrasounds or anything, but because it is free, everything takes time. At first, you will find it frustrating to visit the doctor, but slowly you get used to the processes and start appreciating them. It is worth noting that people have started demanding faster and better healthcare through privatisation.

Your Home

Canada has very different homes from the ones in India. They are mostly independent townhouses with a lot of space in the form of a backyard or a front yard. The houses are lined up picturesquely and look similar to each other but beautiful. They are made of wood and are soundproof, so you don't hear the outside world.

Kitchens come well-equipped. A rented house includes a dishwasher, fridge, microwave oven and washer-dryer by default. And yes, the cooktop is electric. You have to learn the art of cooking on it, as the heating settings are different, but slowly you get used to it.

Other kitchen activities are easier in Canada because of the packaging, which I have discussed already. You get fresh, pre-cleaned and pre-cut vegetables or fruits. There is no need to wash or sort them, which reduces the effort even when you are doing things on your own. In India, we usually rely on our domestic help for things like cleaning, sorting, chopping, etc. This is not required here. You do have to do things on your own, but it is far more convenient. Washing utensils is a challenge but can be easily figured out if you develop the habit of rinsing dishes and putting them in the dishwasher immediately after meals.

Of course, you need to learn about all those machines—which dishwasher is to be used, which utensil shiner, how to clean them, etc. Laundry is also done differently from how it is done in India, as we don't hang clothes to dry them. In Canada, due to the weather, people only use dryers to dry their clothes. Clothes are washed and dried using two big machines that you slowly learn about. If you want to do a cold wash, you have to explicitly choose that setting, because the water is hot by default. This is just one example of the kind of thing you will have to get used to, but all of it can be learnt and the process is better than going through the cycle of hanging clothes and pulling them off the clotheslines.

Heating/air-conditioning is another aspect of life here that you will get used to. The heating in your house will be working non-stop in all kinds of weather, because of which you won't be able to open windows much. You will learn about the concept of a humidifier and the need for it.

But above all, you will love the peace, the sense of security at home and the freedom from the need for domestic help. Along the way, you will learn to make your life easier in many ways. Keeping autobots to clean your house and having cleaning help come over once a week to thoroughly clean the washrooms are some of the life hacks you will pick up.

You will get used to keeping tubs and washrooms dry, as there are no drains. While the experience of living in Canada is completely different, you will love the change.

Roads and Traffic

Roads are free of rash driving. People here religiously follow rules and speed limits. You may encounter traffic at certain hours in the city but you will never have to wait endlessly on the roads. You won't see the police a great deal. No one is keeping watch all the time, as people tend to behave themselves, functioning on trust and good faith. All the old moral values still hold true in Canada. People respect each other's privacy.

Canada's Weather

Canada's weather is as beautiful as a fairy tale and as dangerous as a mountaineering expedition. Even the slightest carelessness can cost you your limb or your life. So Canada has both beauty and danger, but with the right set of clothes, you can enjoy yourself here.

'Weather forecast: Snowfall' will be a daily update on your phone. You will plan going outdoors and spending time indoors according to the weather forecast. Slowly, with time, -5°C will begin to seem warmer to you after you have already seen -35°C. You will also come to love the walks, even when you are wearing a winter jacket. You will have to wear winter clothing almost all the time—jackets, caps, gloves and heavy boots will be part of your daily 'going out' wardrobe. You will start spending on Canadian woollen clothing, realising that Indian winter clothes are not fit for Canadian weather.

You will slowly start learning about and enjoying new terms and phenomena like 'snowfrost', 'diamond dust', and 'twinkling stars'. You won't be able to keep yourself away from the night sky, parks, etc.

Slowly…

… the white beauty of Canada will mesmerise you…

… you will start loving nature again…

… you will start enjoying long forest trails…

… you will get used to parks and outdoor fun, or even indoor fun with hot pools…

… ice skating and sledding will become your favourite pastimes…

… the beauty of snowflakes will inspire you to live your life more beautifully…

Experience Canada @ https://www.youtube.com/@iseecanada3432

Land of Living Skies –

Greens are No Less –

Greens are No Less –

Patience: The Key to Success

You have taken a very big decision in your life, one that will bring a storm of changes to your stagnant boat. Nobody feels comfortable with change and, when it is as massive as moving to a new country, no matter how strong your ship is, you have to navigate the high tide and rough waters with patience.

So be a brave captain of your ship. Use all your skills, have faith in God and do your best. You will surely reach your destination port.

But remember, life is not about the destination. It is about the journey. So, while initially you will face turbulence, emotional trauma, a lack of confidence and the feelings of being lost and missing your loved ones, slowly, after six months or a year, the waters will settle down. The emotional turbulence will go away, and then you will be able to see clearly what your future holds in store for you.

No country is good or bad and no decision is right or wrong. It all depends on you, not the country.

Are you feeling better in the place you have moved to?

Are you feeling more secure?

Is it worth adjusting to the new place?

Are you ready to sacrifice your comfort?

Patience is key. Don't get overwhelmed by the initial hiccups, which are but natural. Even moving from one city to another within the same country requires reorientation. When you are moving across countries, you should not expect an easy pass.

So, rethink your 'why'. Why did you think of moving? Why it is important for you? Can you afford to give up on the 'why' because of which you moved to Canada? For instance, if you moved to Canada hoping that your kids would be stress-free or to prioritise your personal life, are you okay with giving up on that—with taking your kids back to a highly competitive study environment, with compromising on your personal life?

Choose what you can or cannot afford. It's perfectly normal to rethink your needs in life. **Remember, mangos are sweet and so is maple. What you have to decide is which kind of sweetness you want.**

Get hold of your life. Trust your decision and set sail.

List of Items to be Taken from India

Tip 1: To save money, avoid spending as soon as you land (you will get everything in Canada but it is all far more expensive than in India).

Utensils that are Specific to Indian Cuisine

1. *Belan*[26]
2. *Chimta*[27]
3. *Khallad*[28]
4. *Maasal daani*[29]
5. Grater
6. Knife
7. Tea pan
8. Non-stick/iron *tawa*[30]
9. Cooker
10. *Idli*[31] maker

Tip 2: Bring a *papad*[32] roaster to roast *chapati*.[33] As cooktops are generally made of glass in Canada, you will not be able to use them to roast *chapati*.

---

26 Rolling pin
27 Tongs
28 Pastel
29 Spice box
30 Round frying pan
31 South Indian rice cake
32 A deep-fried crunchy Indian batter of black gram bean flour
33 A common Indian flatbread

Tip 3: Bring utensils that have a flat base.

Tip 4: Bring a limited number of cutlery items and plates for the first few days. You may opt for the disposable kind.

Tip 5: Bring dishwasher-safe utensils.

Tip 6: Visit Dollarama or Dollar Tree to buy inexpensive, daily-use household items for the kitchen, for cleaning, etc. Trust me, it will save you a lot of money.

Medicines

1. Basic antibiotics are a must, as you won't get those in Canada without a prescription from a Canadian doctor.
2. Regular medicines that you take for blood pressure, thyroid problems, etc.
3. Generic medicines:

   a. Painkillers
   b. Medicines to prevent vomiting
   c. Medicines for gastric issues
   d. Eucalyptus capsules for steaming
   e. Balm
   f. Volini
   g. Burnol
   h. Eyetone (very expensive in Canada)
   i. Boroline
   j. Sualin
   k. Hajmola
   l. Calcium tablets
   m. Crocin
   n. Allegra

Tip 7: Carry a stock for at least three months, to last you until you get a family doctor.

Spices

It is a good idea to carry the following spices for your first few days:

1. Chilli
2. *Garam masala*
3. *Sambhar masala*
4. *Chole masala*[34]
5. Turmeric
6. Coriander powder

Tip 8: Don't carry any seeds. Seeds are not allowed, so avoid *rai, jira,* etc.

Tip 9: Don't carry salt or sugar or *heeng*[35] or any white stuff, as white powdery substances raise suspicions during security checks. This can add delays to your travels.

Religious Items

1. *Dhoop*[36]
2. *Diya*[37]
3. Cotton
4. Idols
5. Photos
6. Books
7. Camphor

---

34 Items 2, 3 and 4 are Indian spice mixtures.
35 Asafoetida
36 Incense
37 Oil lamps

8. Matchboxes
9. *Roli/moli*

Clothes

Limit yourself to the basics + two or three sets for occasional wear. Carry more items for kids, though. As it is cold in Canada, you will mostly need Canadian jackets, woollens, etc. Inners are useless here, as the interiors of buildings are heated. You need clothes that you can layer and that are easy to pull off when not required.

Gadgets and Chargers

Carry whatever gadgets (laptop, tablet, Alexa, etc.) you have and want to use along with a spare India-to-Canada socket/converter.

Tip 10: Don't buy any new electronic devices or paraphernalia in India, as Canada's standard voltage is different from India's and you get better options in Canada.

Cosmetics

Carry only the bare minimum. Cosmetics are better in Canada, so slowly buy what you need.

Carry Your Gold and Diamonds

While first landing in or entering Canada, you will not be charged any customs duty for your valuables. But if you bring them over later, you will need to pay up. So bring everything with you when you immigrate.

If you plan to bring some stuff later, create a detailed list with photos and estimated costs (it doesn't matter if you don't have the bills). Declare the list of items you will be bringing later. This will also save you from having to pay customs duty.

Eatables

1. Ready-to-eat packets for the first few days
2. *Puri*[38]
3. *Achaar*[39]
4. *Namkeen*[40]
5. *Laddoo*[41]
6. *Mathari*[42]

Miscellaneous

1. Needle and thread
2. Vim bar

Household

1. Quilts
2. Bedsheets

Important Documents

Tip 11: Make two copies of each document.

Tip 12: An international driving licence is not required in Canada.

Tip 13: Bring your driving licence abstract. It will help you get a driving licence in Canada.

1. Original degrees and certificates
2. Original birth certificate
3. Original vaccination card

---

38 Deep-fried bread
39 Pickle
40 Savouries
41 Round Indian sweet
42 Flakey biscuit

4. Kids' latest report cards
5. Temporary one-month smart insurance in case you face any medical emergencies
6. Marriage certificate **in English**
7. Driving licence **in English**
8. Prescriptions for all the medicines you need
9. Proof of funds
10. Cash (up to $10,000)
11. Make a list of all the items in each suitcase. Sample list:

S. No.	Red Suitcase, Large	22 kg
1	Pooja plate with diya	
2	Kapoor/matchbox	
3	Cotton + ghee	
4	Books	
5	Roli/moli/chandan	
6	Dhoop	
7	Grater	
8	Idli maker	
9	Peeler	
10	Knife	
11	Masale daani	
12	Spoon set	
13	Vegetable cutter	
14	Garam masala	
15	Haldi/mirchi/coriander	
16	Sambhar masala	
17	Meat masala	

18	Cockroach gel	
19	Kashmiri mirch	
20	Methi	
21	Chhole masala	
22	Chat masala	
23	Sponge wipe	
24	Laundry bag	
25	Vim bar with scrubber	

S. No.	Blue Suitcase, Large (L)	22 kg
1	Quilts	
2	Dohar	
3	Bedsheets	
4	Pillow covers	
5	Mattress protector	
6	Caps	
7	Socks	
8	Handkerchiefs	

S. No.	Blue Suitcase, Large (S)	16 kg
1	Baby liquid soap/kit	
2	Shampoo	
3	Soap khadi	
4	Rin	
5	Towels (big)	
6	Nail cutter	
7	Moisturiser	
8	Razor	

9	Toothbrushes	
10	Toothpaste	
11	Bindi/earbuds	
12	Facial kit	
13	Sunglasses	
14	UGs Hanu	
15	UGs Man	
16	UGs Woman	
17	T-shirt	
18	Jeans	
19	Jackets	
20	Sweaters	
21	Belts	
22	Socks	

… and so on for each suitcase.

Landing Process – Canada Visa[43]

When to Land

After getting the PR visa, you are supposed to complete your 'landing' on or before the visa expiry date (mentioned on the visa). The visa expiry date is either*:

- One year from the medical tests, or
- The passport expiry date of the Primary Applicant (PA) or any of his/her accompanying dependents

*Whichever of the above two is earlier.

Who Should Land First

It is the obligation of the Primary Applicant to land first, but this can be done along with one or more or all of the accompanying family members.

The Primary Applicant's dependents CANNOT land first.

Procedure at the Port of Entry

Irrespective of the city you choose to land in, the 'landing' itself is a simple process. Before disembarking from the craft, you will be provided with a Disembarkation Card/Form. You need to take that form and go to Passport Control.

---

43 Please note that all of the information in this section has been drawn from official sources and was valid at the time of writing but should be verified by applicants, as these protocols and procedures change with time.

At Passport Control

Here, you need to inform the Immigration Officer (IO) that you have come to complete your 'landing'. The IO will check your Disembarkation Card and your passport/s and visa and then direct you to the Newly Landed Immigrants' Counter.

At the Immigration Counter

Here, the IO will scrutinise your passport/s and COPRs. He or she might (or might not) ask to see your proof of funds (POF). Most of the time, the IO will accept what you say and not count the actual money, but do not attempt any pretensions there. The IO will then fill some portions of the COPR and ask you to sign it, after which it will be attached to your passport. You will be asked to fill in the PR card application form and provide an address to which your PR cards will be forwarded within three to six weeks. Then, the IO will welcome you to Canada and direct you to the Services Canada office.

At the Services Canada Office

The Services Canada section is for assisting newcomers with their settlement. Here, you will get lots of books/pamphlets that will provide you with crucial information on Canada and settlement plans. From here you will be directed to the CBSA counter.

At the CBSA (Customs) Office

This is an important stop. You are required to present:

1. A list of items accompanying.
2. A list of goods to follow.
3. A currency declaration (you need to 'declare' any amount that is greater than $10,000).

You will need to carry two copies of Lists 1 and 2. One copy will be retained by CBSA and the second copy will be returned to you. You will need the second copy when your shipments come in.

NOTE:

- If you are not bringing in any goods later, you don't need the 'goods to follow' list.
- The CBSA might at random 'actually' check the POF here. Thus, no complacency is acceptable.
- If there is jewellery involved, do not forget to bring printed photographs of the same (details later).

Forms Required for the 'Landing'

Even if you stay ONLY for a day at Canada, you will need the following:

1. Passport with stamped visa
2. COPR (IMM 52928)
3. POF
4. Passport-size photos
5. PR Card Application (IMM 5444E). Carry it filled and pre-printed, for ease.
6. Goods Lists (Form B4/B4A). All the goods that you are either carrying on your person ('goods accompanying', as shown in the tables above) or intend to bring at a later date ('goods to follow') need to be listed in form B4/B4A, separately. These forms are available on the CBSA website: **http://www. cbsa.gc.ca/publications/forms-formulaires/b4-eng.pdf**. Club similar items together in groups (e.g. DVDs: Qty-98, Books: Qty-42, etc.). The entire list should be priced against each group and totalled at the end. Carry 'original' invoices for high-end items (this is a must for diamonds). Others can be broadly/generally (but appropriately) priced. Carry these forms filled out and pre-printed, for ease (two copies).

7. Jewellery list, signed by jeweller. Jewellery items MUST be listed and the document should carry photographs of each item. Sort the photos according to the type of jewellery (e.g. rings, necklaces, etc.). Sample as shown

8. Electronics list. Mention the serial numbers.

Sample Jewelry List

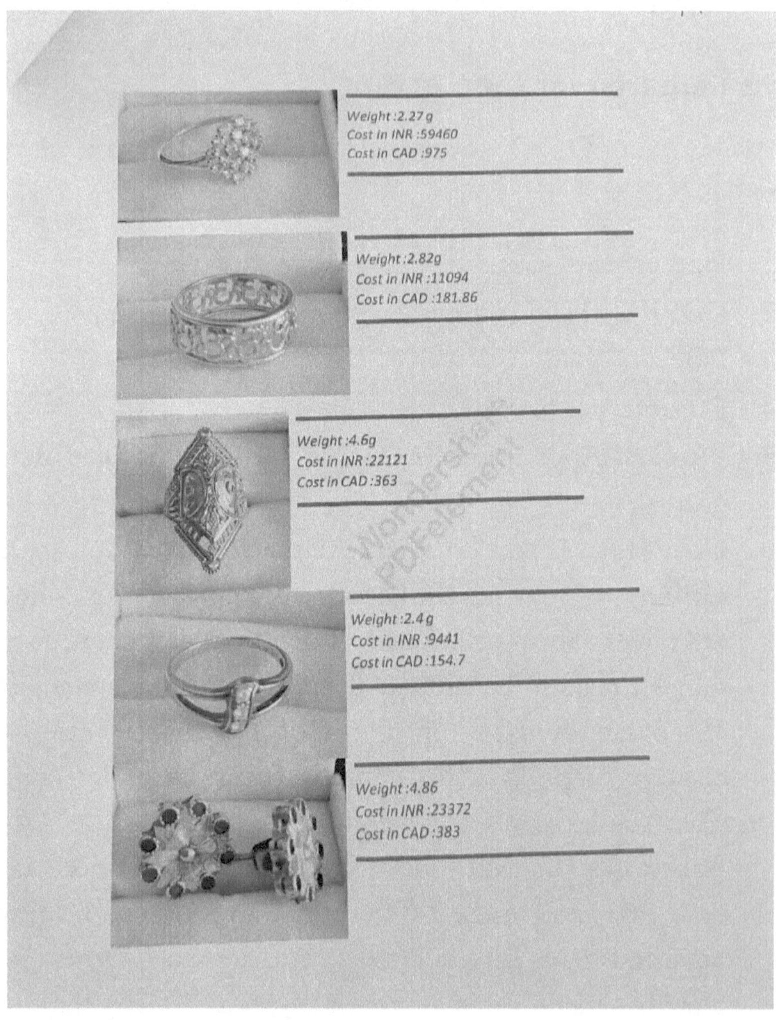

Short-Stay Accommodation

You must arrange a short-stay accommodation prior to your landing. The necessity of this cannot be over-emphasised. If you have friends/relatives, they can be approached for the same. If you do not have anyone, book an Airbnb or a hotel room.

Money

What Proofs Are Acceptable?

If you are carrying more than $10,000, inform a Canadian official when you arrive in Canada. If you do not tell an official, you may be fined or put in prison. These funds can be in the form of cash, securities in bearer form (e.g. stocks, bonds, debentures, treasury bills, etc.) or negotiable instruments in bearer form (e.g. bank drafts, cheques, TCs or MOs). Source: **http://www.cic.gc.ca/english/immigrate/skilled/funds.asp.**

How Much Can You Carry?

There is no upper limit. You can take millions if you can prove legitimate sources and declare any amount greater than $10,000 (that's the CBSA regulation).

There is a lower limit though. You must carry at least the amount stipulated by the CIC according to the number of accompanying members in your family.

Tax and Duties Component

The funds you bring into Canada are non-taxable. It is only the 'interest' earned on them that is taxed. The moment your funds start accruing interest (while lying in a Canadian bank account), the bank will start deducting tax 'at source'. The same applies in the case of any investment that you make in Canada with these funds.

PR Cards (PRC)

Your PR card application (IMM 5444E) will be done at the POE. It is part of the PR package (free) and the photos and details will be the same as were supplied by you for the PR. Your PR card/s are delivered to you by regular mail in three to six weeks (the average is four weeks). It is advisable to stay in Canada for at least 45 days, collect your PRC and then return if you must.

If you leave the country before your PRC arrives, you will have to make arrangements for its collection and forward delivery to you through a friend/relative. This is not recommended. Although it is attempted all the time by people, there is a danger of losing it in transit. And if that happens, you will have to go through the tedious process of getting a new one made.

If needs to apply later somehow PR Card Application Procedure → http://www.cic.gc.ca/english/pdf/kits/guides/5445E.PDF

NOTE: The PRC is probably the most important document you own after you are done with your PR application process. It is valid for five years. It is free the first time; renewals cost $50/card.

Temporary Health Coverage

It is wise to obtain 'temporary' health coverage before you fly. (This is not required if you are going to Alberta or Manitoba.) This temporary coverage comes in the form of travel insurance, which you can obtain from any insurance company in your home country. The cost depends on the coverage period. Usually, you should purchase a plan for three to four months, as that is the waiting time for health cards in all provinces.

NOTE: It's a good idea to obtain travel insurance from your home country for two reasons:

1. You are covered from day one, even before you land.

2. In Canada, it will be costlier and you'll be covered only from the day you apply. What if you only get to it later, as you'll be busy in the initial days? What if something goes wrong before that?

Things You May Not Like about Canada

1. Canada depends heavily on Canada Post, which is used for most communications.
2. Giving and asking for tips are very common. You will be asked for tips everywhere—in cabs, salons, for anything service-based. The final choice of whether to tip or not is yours.
3. Deliveries are a pain:

   a. Amazon deliveries are left at the door. They don't do handovers, so you have to keep track of your parcel and pick it up.
   b. Amazon returns have to be done by you. You have to drop off your parcels at a Canada Post office.
   c. One only attempt is made to deliver items to your house. If you are not at home, you have to pick up the item from the office of the delivery service.
   d. Even furniture deliveries do not happen on the same day or within two days. They take their own time and have to be pre-booked.

4. You may not like gloomy winter days on which you have to be indoors all the time.
5. You have to do everything on your own, from filling your car with diesel and air to assembling furniture.
6. You have to do household chores every day. Tip: you can hire biweekly cleaning professionals.

7. In severe winters, due to heavy snowfall, snow shovelling can be very painful. **Tip: you can hire someone.**

8. Nobody asks whether you want tea or coffee in stores or shops, even when you go to buy a car. Get used to it.

9. You have to throw the trash out yourself. There are bins that you have to place outside on the days when they are scheduled to be picked up.

10. Homelessness in downtown areas. Usually, downtown is where homeless people roam. You can easily tell.

11. The service industry is not as good as India's, so you may miss the pampering.

12. Your rental is at the mercy of your landlord, so you may struggle to get a rental. There are formal move-in and move-out inspections that cost a lot.

13. Not many vegetarian options.

14. You may not like to wait to see a doctor or to get a test scheduled.

Quick Links

Experience Canada → https://www.youtube.com/@iseecanada3432

Apply for a health card → https://skhealthcard.health.gov.sk.ca/

Access your health records → https://www.ehealthask.ca/mysask healthRecord/MySaskhealthReacord

Get your identity card → https://sgi.sk.ca/photo-id

School registration and Newcomer Student Centre → https://www. saskatoonpublicschools.ca/registration/noncanadian/NSC/Pages/ default.aspx

All about driving's licence, car, motor insurance → https://www. mysgi.ca/

Rental sites:

- https://www.kijiji.ca/
- https://www.zumper.com/
- https://www.broadstreet.ca/
- https://www.bwalk.com/
- https://www.hazelviewproperties.com/

Open a bank account from India and transfer funds before landing → https://straight.scotiobank.com/newcomers.html

Saskatchewan River